I0435889

2014

Global Financial Super Heating

In my attempt to look forward in time and see what is to come for us all, I opened my creative mind completely to any and all possibilities, as should you. The byproduct of that complete opening process sometimes takes me down paths that you, the reader, may wonder why. But look closely as to what seeds may be planted. Some satire may detract from the urgency found within my words, but sarcasm is just a part of my process of thinking and should be accepted as such. Humor is a sign of intelligence and satirical humor is very much part of me. To remove this just goes against my grain for I feel all was meant to be within this book, for it came to me as a part of the creating process of this book and belongs nowhere else. I let the historical information lead me into this future of death staring down at us all, as we all remain seemingly powerless to react. I ask you to accept it (humor) as merely the opening of all avenues within this ever changing forward thinking process of my mind, as it looks into the devastating future of life on earth we all seem to face – a future that looks to be just moments away.

William J. Ryan

Global Financial Super Heating

2014

Written by

William J. Ryan

Illustrated by

William J. Ryan

Global Financial Super Heating

--- FIRST EDITION ---

About the author

You, the reader, should know I am an autodidact (self-directed learner) and I am dyslexic and not only suffer from letters, numbers and spelling of words changing on me, but structuring of sentences will sometimes be backwards.

I do enjoy writing and creating stories and I have written several books (see back pages) but each has been very hard to complete and they take me much longer than you who are not dyslexic. I think my joy of completing one would be that much greater than someone who is normal.

Because parts of this book are fact based I made many discoveries along the way that opened up my mind to our future and any way I looked at it, it's not good and that may be hard for some to read. But read it you should to prepare for what is to come.

I think I see the world through different eyes and may see the world in ways others don't. I see a future that is very bleak and I offer solutions that an independent, healthy overview of religion must be applied to make these solutions possible.

Introduction

In my efforts to write this book I discovered what happened to the **Greatest Generation**. Those men and women that fought in *World War II* and so many paying with their lives so we could be free, or so the theory goes.

This book is the author's personal viewpoints of the devastation and destruction that happens when **one or more** asinine **religions from the dark ages** are permitted to take over a government and kill those who would stand in their godly way, bringing us all back into those days when we needed help ridding the planet of witches and demons.

The founding fathers of this country knew what life was like living under the ignorant evil carnage that is God and did their best to protect us from that insanity. For a short time it worked but that time is gone and as I write these words the First Amendment of the Constitution has been circumvented. No longer do we enjoy **Separation of Church and State** as one religion, the **Christian Supreme Court** made it null and void just this year, 2014, based on news reports.

Most of the time we can see the future, if we just take the time to look into the past, only this time we all are about to witness changes that have never happened before and that makes it hard to envision what is to come. Yet, from where I sit, it is to come and it is to be very bad, regardless of any god.

The experts seem to lean toward the effects of global warming as something to come in a far off distant time, one hundred years, or more, from now and lead you to believe *"all things are fine, don't worry, just keep doing what you are doing."* While others predict nothing will happen and this is all normal changes on the planet Earth. But now most are leaning towards the worst we should see will be nothing more than coastal flooding and a few degrees warmer temperatures. I strongly disagree.

I see the future effects of global *disregard* and *utopian life styles for all,* crashing head on into Mother Nature's revenge. These catastrophic changes are coming at us much faster than the money people predictions we have been told and I believe this pending disaster is linked to paper **money** and **religion.**

The reckless disregard of our financial stability occurs in every country within the current system of today's markets. And the relentless spreading of ancient, barbaric, prehistoric, ignorant, backwater, goat herding gods over one another, is now overlapping borders and crashing into each other with deadly violence, all of which will bring about what I have called *Global Financial Super Heating.*

Things are in place to instill *their* (the 85 richest people in the world –see page 307) peace and total control over us clueless Americans. As these true rulers show *their* power the constitution will disappear before our eyes. These *85* that pick our presidents and hold up the only god to be for us, stand safely behind it all,,, and must be appeased.

Please note:

This book is written in very simple terms to attempt to make sense out of the lies being told to the masses, over thousands of years, by people in positions of power and trust, like religious and government leaders.

Points will be briefly covered and **it is up to YOU, the reader, to verify this information,** as well as expand **YOUR** knowledge on these subjects within.

Had I gone into greater depth, this book would be finished in tiny print, on 8.5" X 11" paper and 4" thick and you would not read it. Most speakers will tell you they must repeat things three times to get their points across because you only hear approximately 40% of what they are saying. It seems to be the best our brains can do even when you read,,, thanks to speed reading.

Therefore I have tried to keep it to the point and simple, repeating my points occasionally three or more times to drive them home for the speed readers and those that **THINK,,, while they READ,,, believing they are getting it all,,,,,,,, but you're not.**

I don't believe we have much time to prepare for what is to come. If you think you are safe living out in the woods, think again, this is coming for us all…. hard and fast. Nothing like what destruction that is to come has ever happened before in the history of earth or man and it will be with us for a long time as the population is destined to decrease in size.

The information found within is limited to my abilities and the constrictions of the powers that control all and our future.

Please also note I have used punctuation marks in unconventional ways to get the reader to STOP AND THINK about what you are reading.

Global Financial Super Heating

Chapter One

Where Are We Now?

Global Financial Super Heating

We people currently on this earth, are most likely well past the top capacity this planet can sustain and are at lightning speed using up all the resources this earth has and had to offer. This is what happens when one species overruns all others with no regard for their effects on the surrounding environment.

The American Indians said it best. *"We must all live together with respect for **all** life around us."* But we don't. We take whatever we want now, with no regards for the future and the next generation coming. Our value systems have changed and it seems the value we place on paper circumvents the value we place on life. All life!!!

Some American Indian cities were estimated to be over 50,000 people and they lived and worked together with all life. Yet slowly over thousands of years, we humanoids were leaving our footprint and extinctions started to grow. It seems that peoples' need for food started to circumvent life as there became more human mouths to feed.

Then along came the European invaders of the new land they named America (not Columbus) and the raping of this land started as though there was no end to the resources. The indigenous people of South America were mostly wiped out from diseases brought from the foreigners and then they were enslaved to harvest and bring back **Spanish** gold and silver to these new kings and under the pretexts of their **new gods**.

The truth is most of this was Inca and Aztec gold and silver. Why to this day, they the Christian invaders, still claim it as theirs, is beyond me. Maybe it's because those Christian-led governments have sold their soul to Satan and in place of love have a bottomless pit they try to fill with greed for money, wealth and power over other people. Is this all part of God's plan? I just don't see love,,, only an imagine of a smiling red horned beast with hooves and a pointy tail and the smell of sulfur. That is if you believe in all that crap.

The original gods of this conquered land were destroyed, as well as their written words; and those people were given a new god, for the king of Spain knew the only way to control people was through God. So it was to be, *"worship our God Christ, your savior, or we will cut off your arms"*,,, and they did. **It is said,,, they did this because they could.**

After approximately five hundred years of European Christian enslavement and total disregard for the environment, while spreading their god's words, we came to the last century. By now, *"Go forth, be fruitful and multiply."* was taking its toll on the land and other life forms. But the word of this horned beast god and others, was spreading and the powers to be were becoming rich off of this god business. So what if a few fellow creatures are hunted to extinction, as long as these **Gods of Prey** are making money? That is God's plan,,, right? Take their land, enslave and kill the people and all life found there, then leave it as a waste land,,, some god.

Gods of Prey and the food chain

If we look at a *food chain pyramid of life,* (Page 19) we can see it is divided up into several groups. Each is endlessly trying to grow to its full potential and spread the joy of its experience as far as it can reach in life.

1. **Bacteria** at the low end.
2. **Plants**
3. **Herbivores**
4. **Carnivores** at the top.
5. **Gods of Prey** above all (Page 22)

All living and surviving together side by side until one gets out of balance and overtakes the others. It has been theorized that the dinosaurs were wiped out because of a bacteria found in their blood and not just a meteorite. This bacteria was infesting herds that were covering the globe and killing everything in sight for their own growth and gains - **or because they could.**

Each one of these have the power to kill and do so and show us all their strength built within their level. From the smallest to the largest, killing is a byproduct of living.

Only one on this chart is not real and yet for some,,, no I fear for most,,, this imaginary deity is the master of all fate that lays before us. It is sad to think such power is given to one over all the others and as it turns out is not even real.

This is a cancerous illness passed on from one generation to the next with a vengeance and will not ever end until we stand up to it and point out the lunacy that is god to all that follow. This madness has a name and there is help for those lost in its religious grip.

It is called **Scrupulosity** and is a taught psychological disorder of the mind passed on from one to the other. This highly contagious disease of the mind holds with it a very high price one must pay for a cure,,, isolation from the pack.

Food Chain Pyramid of Life

This last chart is Mother Nature's plan of the past, lacking modern changes. Therefore I have provided a more detailed category to the next, more current pyramid of life revealing what is above and behind the gods. (Page 22)

In the last 500 plus years the extinction rate of life has been growing much worse and as of 2014 we have managed to extinguish from this life, many of our companions of this thin and very rare space that seems to exist nowhere else. That balance of which has permitted each of us to exist next to each other for millions of years. That balance is now **gone** and the outcome of such ignorance and greed on our part following the **Gods Of Prey** will result in only one type of outcome that I can think of,

influenza.

This great balancer of life is long overdue. Reportedly influenza outbreaks come in 30 year cycles. But with the advances of medications in the last 100 years diseases have been holding back the wave of death that is to come. That and religion permitted an outbreak of people to blossom and grow without regulation. At some point a new influenza (or some type of micro organism like Ebola) will pop up and in seven days will cross the globe. Only those with the strongest constitutions will survive to live once more in the dark ages that are to come. Balance once more will happen, but too late for so many now extinct and this world will have changed, reeling in pain from the reckless disregard for all life taken from us by the **Gods of Prey** (God's of all religions).

But even the power of influenza to clean the globe of this destructive parasite called man, will not stop what is to come. If we all stopped using fossil fuel today,,, it is too late to stop what is coming. This devastation is as close as the next turn of a page in this book,,,

Global Financial Super Heating.

In the next life pyramid chart, I will show how this devastation can happen when one species grows unchecked and uncontrolled. Its herds covering the globe, consuming all in its wake, without regard for others, including the imaginary **Gods of Prey** and their almighty dollars.

Hard to believe that in the past 1000 years the planet's population has grown from about 300 million to 7 billion as of 2010. For me this comical look forward by the number crunchers see the population reaching near 9 billion by 2050 (that is 35 years from now) and topping off at about 9.7 billion by 2150 (per some estimates).

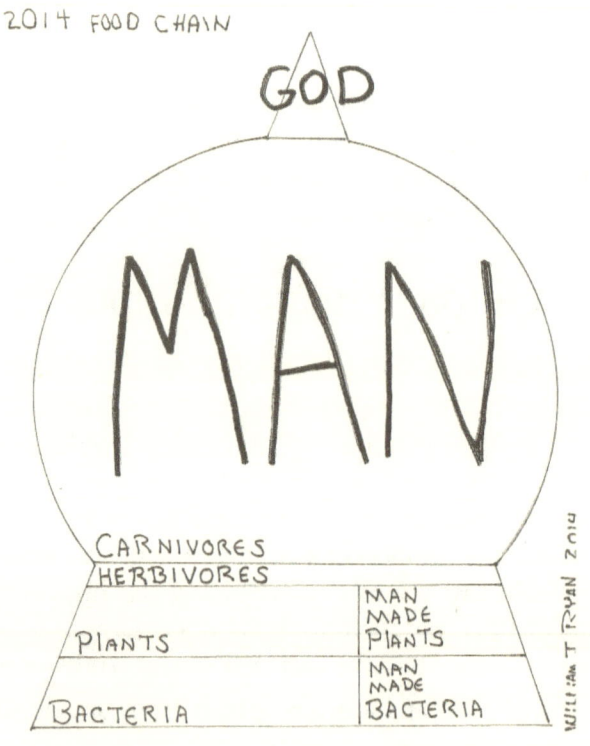

The Man Bulge and his gods.

Global Financial Super Heating

I do not see any of these mathematical approximations coming true because the number crunchers have not looked at the cause and effect of **Global Financial Super Heating** that is just on the horizon. They have not looked at how we have cut down every tree to grow food to feed the masses and now have run out of land to grow more food.

How will we feed the new ones to come, let alone the ones here now, if there is **just one blight**? Just one blight will create such **CHAOS** the likes of which will crush your feelings of security and safety like you have never experienced before in your life.

The rain forests of South America are now a giant farm to mostly grow one food (soybeans that are in all most everything) and one of the great air conditioners (the rain forest) of this planet is now for the most part,,, **gone**. The top soil is thin there and will not sustain our needs as it too is washed into the sea, as the Great Plains in North America has seen. We are at the top of our planet's food growth curve and per the United Nations, "*food production will slow over the next ten years and the costs will rise.*" Food will be a thing for the rich, while the poor starve. And I am sure they are not taking into account the crash of the dollar and other global currencies, that is to come and how it will play into the future.

Plus the war on abortion has had its overwhelming effects. We don't look at that, because over 2.5 billion people follow the teachings of one of these antiquated, global, suicidal, babbling **Gods of Prey**. All at the destructions of the rest of life and they are joined by the other *onlookers* that do nothing or say nothing because it is God's will,,, so it must be ok. Or it is because they who stand behind these gods are so rich and powerful that none of us can stop them and survive their revenge.

Their power is so strong that news of these upcoming calamities is never permitted to leak out to the masses. That would be bad for the god business and they may see revenues drop. **They do it because they can.**

At this same time we have harvested from the seas,

over 90%

of all the fish in the world, to feed the masses up to this point and the remaining food in the oceans will not sustain the level of people here now, let alone the ones to come per the number crunchers. Off the coast of Africa the seas have been stripped so clean of food by the great ships of the rich countries, for **their people**, that the African people trying to live there, now hunt the wild life inland,,, to extinction,,, for food. There are great sections of land if not countries that have lost most if not all of their wild life. **Gone!!!**

"The future for these remaining animals lies within zoos." Words to this effect, were said by the

creator of the first zoo in England in the 1800s. Growing up as a kid I thought he was nuts. Today, we can all see what he could envision over 100 years earlier.

The following is a short list, of extinct birds and is not complete by any means. I only wish to show how man's foot print is crushing other life and there is much more that is lost if you look up extinct animals. There is a mind numbing number gone for good. How could this ever be any part of God's plans?

Extinguished Birds

1. Chiffchaff   1986
        Canary Islands
2. Alaotra Grebe   1985
        Madagascar
3. Aldabra Bush-warbler   1983
        Seychelles
4. Cyprus Dipper   1950
        Cyprus
5. Arabian Ostrich   1942
        Middle East
6. Canary Island Oystercatcher   1940
        Spain
7. Ryukyu Wood Pigeon   1936
        Japan
8. Mukojima White eye   1930
        Japan

Global Financial Super Heating

9. Madeiran Wood Pigeon   1924
        Portugal
10. Bonin Nankeen Night Heron   1889
        Japan
11. Bonin Wood Pigeon   1889
        Japan
12. Ryukyu Kingfisher   1887
        Japan
13. Seychelles Parakeet   1886
        Seychelles
14. Newton's Parakeet   1875
        Mauritius
15. Reunion Starling   1850
        France
16. Spectacled Cormorant   1850
        Russia
17. Mauritius Owl   1850
        Mauritius
18. Mascarene Parrot   1834
        France
19. Delalande's Coua   1834
        Madagascar
20. Mauritius Blue Pigeon   1830
        Mauritius
21. Bonin Grosbeak   1827
        Japan
22. Bonin Thrush   1827
        Japan
23. Mauritius Grey Parrot   1764
        France

Global Financial Super Heating

24. Rodrigues Night Heron	1750
Mauritius	
25. Reunion Gallinule	1730
France	
26. Reunion Flightless Ibis	1720
France	
27. Red Rail	1710
Mauritius	
28. Reunion Pigeon	1705
France	
29. Mascarene Coot	1693
Mauritius	
30. Mauritian Duck	1690
France	
31. Mauritian Shelduck	1690
France	
32. Mauritius Night-Heron	1690
Mauritius	
33. Broad-billed Parrot	1680
Mauritius	
34. Dodo	1662
Mauritius	
35. Ascension Flightless Crake	1656
United Kingdom	

Global Financial Super Heating

I am willing to bet you did not read each one of their names. They and their lives, valued so little that you can't take a moment out of your life, to just read their names, let alone look up and see what they once were, when they lived and how they once shared this same place with the rest of us in this slender blue strip of time and space.

It's only a thin layer over the top of the skin of this single planet that we all share and we just don't seem to stop killing everything in sight as quickly as possible,,, for Gods' sakes. As though there was some race to cut down every tree, kill every living thing so they, Mr. and Mrs. Gadget, can have one of everything. I am reminded of an educated young women I once knew. She summed it up best, *"The one that has all the toys at the end,,, wins."* Needless to say, she is no longer in my life. But these people are out there and this is their view. This is how they think, this is how they are educated and this is how they live. *"God wants all people to be rich and have one of everything."*

I feel it is a good thing we are the only form of intelligent life we can find in the universe. For if we could find more we would kill it, eat it, or poison it through our own ignorance with the **Gods of Prey** to help. Mother Nature may be very smart indeed for she may have isolated us all from other forms of live to ensure we cannot destroy them as well, with our ignorance.

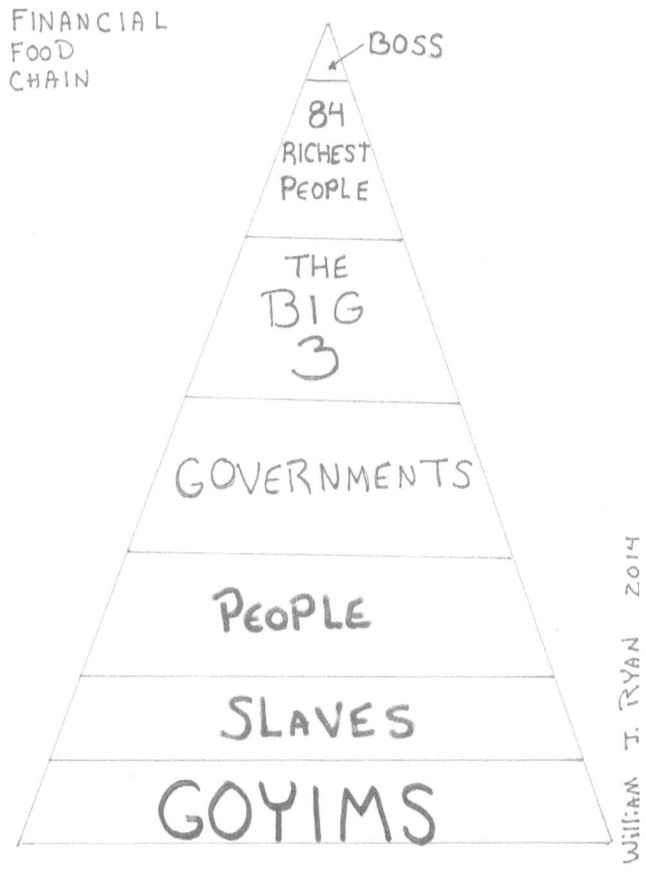

Global Financial Super Heating

Chapter Two

Crash of the Dollar

Trillion Dollar Coin

In God we trust

There is no way we who live on this planet can avoid what is to come. In the past other countries have experienced the same train wreck we are about to have but this one will be much worse, unlike any before. Allegedly the major global financial markets have trusted the United States dollar from the end of World War II and today they are starting to back away.

Currency at one time was a real thing, gold and silver. Something we all could trust to be safe and above the ever shrinking paper dollar that now covers the globe. The federal government has kindly provided us with an estimated devaluing value of the Federal Reserve note and that is 3% each year, even though they will deny this fact. So your saving must pay 3% per year just to keep even with what it was worth a year ago.

Global Financial Super Heating

I use the U.S. Department of Health and Human Services numbers printed annually from their poverty guidelines. These numbers only go back to 1982 when apparently we did not have poverty before then. They suggest that a family of 4 could live on $9,300.00 in 1982 and that same family today would only need $23,850.00. **That is 256% over the past 32 years.** If you work out the numbers of the true cost of living, each person in this family, after paying rent and utilities, would have to live on $2.00 per day for food, not buy clothes, not have health insurance, and not have any other basic necessities. You do it,,, work out the numbers and try to work, feed, provide a home, and care for this family of four on those dollars. You can't unless you keep them in a cardboard box in the woods.

The government has a nice name for this predisposition and ever shrinking dollar and that is the term,,, inflation.

There is no such thing as inflation!

Get your head out of this trickery and look at what is really happening. Things don't go up in value,,, paper money goes down in value,,, it takes more **paper dollars** to buy the same things!

This planned devaluing currency they called inflation is a nice way to put positive spin on a negative fact. Inflation sounds a lot better than devaluation of your hard earned money. But this is how it works. Like I said, at one time money was based on a real thing. Take a $20.00 gold piece printed in 1865. Now if you can imagine holding this coin in your hand for moment and look at it. What is it? It is just a lump of hard metal stamped into a round flat cylinder. Each year this metal disk requires more and more of their paper dollars to buy one.

As it sits there over the years in your hand, did it grow in size? Does it now weight more? Did production of gold stop and has this one metal disk become more rare? No it is just a flat round disk of metal that in its day would buy you about the same goods then as it would now. The only thing that has changed is how many slips of paper it takes to get one. **It,,,** that hunk of gold has not changed,,, the value of paper has changed!

Price of gold
The following values are approximates

In 1775 a new country created its own paper money and called it Continental Currency. The founding fathers were indeed clever and on a paper bill from May, 1775 is written, ***"This bill entitles the bearer to receive five Spanish milled dollars, or the value thereof in gold or silver,,,"***. Sounds good, right? Paper backed with real metal.

Now did you catch the **legal trickery**? They were with us then as they are with us now. The founding fathers knew the new currency would sink like a rock in water so they put *"or the value thereof in gold or silver."* Five dollars of gold or silver would have weighed more in 1775 than it would weigh in 2014. Attorneys!!!!

Then apparently this new country ran out of gold and silver to back their new currency (paper money) and under another name, a bill is written *"According to a resolution of congress passed at Philadelphia February 17, 1776."* Was this our first federal reserve note,,, backed by nothing? Allegedly one of the founding fathers was said to say something like, *"This is one of the best things we ever did."*, referring to the printing of money with nothing to back it. Is not that counterfeit money and fraud and would this be the part that Christians claim when they say *"America was founded on good Christian beliefs"*?

The oldest American record I can find for the price of gold is dated 1792 and at that time one could buy an ounce of gold for just under $20.00 (approximate value 19.40). The next price I can find is in 1850 (58 years later) and the price of gold at that time was approximately $18.90. Before, during, and after the American civil war this metal remained stable and did not change in value. At the beginning of WWI was the first time the dollar started to shrink in value and by 1919 (just after WWI) gold would cost around $19.90.

By the depression of the late 1920s, gold saw a dip from about $20.65 to $17.00 and in 1934 rose to $33.70. As we entered WWII the value remained virtually the same (1945 $34.70).

Reserve currencies (a nice name for fake money or counterfeit because it is backed with nothing but the government's word) have come and gone and it seems a government cannot grow and survive without constant injections of this narcotic. For this country the need for lots of cash may have started when the first state corporation was able to move across state lines and amass larger and larger fortunes creating the new **American Interests**.

After WWII a system for global money was established called the Bretton Woods System and was accepted by the international financial community. The United States dollar was to become the anchor of this global currency need and replaced one of the world financial anchors, the Pound Sterling (English money).

"In God We Trust" appears on the first coin in 1864 as the American war-torn country is split apart. Then in 1955 (gold value was $35.00) the government passed a law to have **"In God We Trust"** printed on paper money and it appeared in 1957 on paper currency. Why would a government do such a thing? Is it because God has taken over the government or could it be **they** (the power behind God and government) saw what was to come and the need to build **faith** in the paper currency as they did at the end of the Civil War and who better than GOD,,, any god would do,,, creating the Almighty Dollar.

Global Financial Super Heating

Throughout the military coup of 1963 (the assassination of John F. Kennedy) and all the race riots, the dollar remained somewhat stable and that same year saw the first **Federal Reserve Note.** The price of gold remained about the same, just under $35.00 until 1967 (4 years) when it took more US falling paper dollars, or notes, to buy gold. The race was on to spend these notes as fast as the government could print them and they still had the pretense of value,,, like coins do today.

This is when the government was in high gear replacing the real gold and silver backed paper money with **god/notes** and the true value of these notes started to show their ugly head. The Vietnam War was cranking up (thanks to Lyndon Johnson, a Christian) and as the government is printing more and more **god/notes** they started to deplete their value (go figure). That is to say if it is possible for a paper note (IOU) backed by God, can have any value, but the god people think so (hence the support of religion).

Think what a great scam has been pulled on the American people by a corrupt military government wanting to expand under the pretense of protecting this country from the Boogie Man. What better means than to create **Gods Notes** to fool the masses. Like the Spanish, they use God to control people while each power player gets what they want, a piece of the action. The weapons manufacturers get to charge any price they want building endless war supplies that **must** be used.

Global Financial Super Heating

The military get to have all the fun of invading countries and killing people that they (the American military) love so much to do. Private companies get to rebuild what the war mongers destroyed and the Christians get to spread the word of their god over others, (all the non-Christians that have just been devastated), all at the expense of the American tax paying people that get left holding the bag of debt. Our hard earned dollars end up in the hands of the people behind the government and behind God.

Then came the oil crises where the Saudi Arabian dictatorship stopped the production and selling of oil and the markets start to crash. It should be noted the OPEC nations only stopped selling to Canada, Japan, the United Kingdom and, of course, America because of the Yom Kippur War in October of 1973. This war involved Egypt and Syria as it was their plan to invade Israel and regain Arab territories lost in 1967. Gold saw a price hike from 1970 to 1975, in just 5 years climbing from $36.00 to $160.00, or about 450%. Did the U.S. dollar **god/note** drop in value more than 75% with respect to gold because of oil? Over the next 26 years the price of gold rose about 170% to $270.00 in 2001 (or the **god/note** lost about 43%) and remained relatively stable until September 11, 2001.

From that year to 2007 (about 5 years) the price of gold climbed to near $700.00 or the price of the devaluing dollar made the cost of the metal climb by over 250% in this short time, (or the **god/note** saw over 60% reduction in value). Then came the big crash of 2007 and to the year of 2011 we saw gold peak at around $1,600.00 and now (2014) it is dropping and is around $1,300.00. This makes the percent of declining dollar almost 190% in 7 years (or over 45% reduction in value).

Recap; 1835 to1913 the price of gold was stable and remained virtually unchanged for 78 years. Four wars, 50 years and one military coup later, the price of gold doubled. Printing of the **god/notes** and the price of gold rose a staggering 3,700% in just the last 50 years. This is why I say, you don't want to keep your money, in money.

So who cares?

Why should we care if a government knows paper money is designed to decrease in value and this is built into **their** system? They are probably very happy to have you accept 95% value on paper it runs out of its printing presses each year. That is a lot better than its true value,,, 0% because it is a note, not backed with anything real. But don't tell anyone,,, it's a government secret. That is why they preach at us to save, save, save and don't spend that worthless **god/note**,,, it makes theirs more valuable. Now think about that!

The government can print as much money as it wants and like us - we are exempt from any responsibility for spending money we don't have, right? After all if our checking account starts to get low, all we need do is add a few zeros and the account is full again. Isn't that how we all live? No wait, we don't live that way and the money must be in the account first before we spend it, otherwise we will just bounce checks all over town and no one will take our checks anymore. We are isolated from everyone and not trusted. <u>That is how it works.</u>

But the United States government (or the ones behind it) can add new zeros to its checking account balance by just passing new laws creating new money or more **god/notes**. There is a new law being considered to go on the books that will eliminate the government's debt completely,,, 100% gone over night.

This law is intended to do just that, add zeros to the governments checking account balance. They just need to mint trillion dollar coins and put them in the bank. We are 17 trillion dollars in debt, (as of this year we are told) so they need only stamp out 17 coins,

"cur chink"

and like that,,, the debt is gone. So why worry? Overnight we will no longer be running a deficit and we will be debt free. Wouldn't that be nice if we all could do that? But printing money or the **god/notes** on our own is against some law I am sure.

Global Financial Super Heating

At the end of WWII the International Monetary Fund and others formed a type of World Bank to stabilize paper money printed in all countries. Sometimes called the Bretton Woods System, became the standard by which we all trust paper money. It all is just paper with ink on it. I think of them (each country in this system) as one drunk leaning on the other.

Other countries have tried to print their way out of debt before and we have seen them crash and crash hard for many years. Yes printing money will pay off our debts and when the investors get this bogus money or **god/notes** they will spend it as fast as they can, running up the price of everything. Much like the stock market did when it got a hold of your 401K **god/notes**. The stock did not grow in value it just had more of your money and drove up the price of the stock creating a bubble. The value of your 401K dollars will drop in value as you and others put more and more of your money (spend it) into this bubble all at risk.

All stock as I understand, is a piece of a real business, real building, real property and real things that have a set value. Overnight they don't just go up in value,,, but layman perceptions do. The influx of all that cash, has deflated its (your cash) value. Those 401k dollars drop in value because it takes more and more dollars to buy stock. Stock is not going up in value,,, your dollars are dropping in value as more and more of you invest.

Global Financial Super Heating

Think of what I am saying, the government prints paper and **you** give it value. They want you to save these paper money **god/notes** so it holds up the illusion of value as they spend theirs as fast as they can. You then put that paper in a box and don't spend it, (savings, checking, safe deposit box, under your bed) making all other paper money more valuable. When one spends the paper, it brings down the value of all paper money and it takes more paper to buy the same thing. That is the stock market. Anything over its true value is hype, air, blue sky and all at risk.

As I understand, stocks remained flat (around 1000) from the 1960s to the early 1980s when 401k money started to come in. For twenty years it rose until the year 2000 (over 10,000 points) and today (2014) it is at or near 16,000.

Now if we use the government's own numbers for the devaluing of the U.S. dollar applied to the poverty guidelines, over the past 32 years,,, the dollar has dropped in value by 61%. Or you would need to find a 1982 dollar and multiply it by 256% to equal its devaluing value for today. We now apply this same devaluing amount to the stock market in 1982 and the stock market should be at 2,560. Yes I know new stocks have been added but not that much in real value. Stocks like internet stock are mostly all blue sky and have no real value. This could be why we see such hard fluctuations in value, because they, who invest all the time, are in the know and are looking for the other shoe to drop (the next crash they know is coming).

The national debt remained flat from 1945 to the 1970 and doubled in the next 10 years or so. In 1982 the debt was just over one trillion. If we apply the same percentages of devaluing to those dollars the debt should be just over three trillion. But we are at 17 trillion equaling around 1,450%.

This exercise is only to show how long of a limb we have all stepped out on to. Money has no value and if you spent it at this rate, the crash that is coming will be very hard. You can see how the clock is running out on paper money. <u>It has no value if you spend it like it has no value</u>, and this government is, has and will continue to spend with the true power players well entrenched behind it.

However because we are all linked together via the World Banks (one drunk leaning on another) when we go, we will take other countries with us that have loaned us money. It is going to be one big global crash. Unless all the drunks shore up the biggest drunk of all,,, America and we all keep pretending paper money is real, like the Kings Clothes.

There seems to be only two ways of running this Christian-led government: 1) print more paper money or the trillion dollar platinum coins, or 2) raise the countries borrowing limit, the debt ceiling. For you and me there is another way,,, just stop spending money. If we don't have any money most of us stop. Most of us live within a budget and don't start endless wars with our neighbors, and using the justification that we are spreading the word of God. But the ignorant do, as well as those suffering from SCRUPULOSITY. Those people are still living in the dark ages, holding on to their pathetic gods, as they make adjustments in the old book of God, to fit new information that runs the masses as they holds on to the money cow,,, the religious. All hand in hand with the ever growing war profiteers,,, any excuse to kill. They are all being played.

All we need do is look to the past and we can see other countries that have tried to print their way out of debt. It did not work in the past and it will not work now,,, but it may be coming soon to a bank near you.

Reportedly Germany financed World War I and assumed massive debt. **Sounds like America**. The time was about 1919 that their dollar starting falling. At that point hyperinflation took hold of the mark and coins and small currency became valueless, (like today in America). The German government started printing 50 million dollar banknotes in 1923. At this time it had shifted into super hyperinflation. Now remember there is no such thing as inflation so this is what I call, super hyper-devaluation of paper money. **<u>The worst place you can have your money is in money.</u>**

Another bungling way to mismanage our currency is to just write it down. That sounds good. We can pay back our debts with smaller dollars. If

Global Financial Super Heating

you have bought a $10,000.00 United States Treasury note and hope to gain 0.25% interest over the next ten years and the government writes down the dollar by 25%,,, over night your money, all American money, has shrunk by that amount. Your $10,000.00 note is now worth $7,500.00,,, overnight. You will still get back your $10,000.00 only it will buy only $7,500.00 worth of goods.

Your food will cost more by that percent or higher. Gasoline will climb by the same percent or more as panic races across the globe. If you are on the edge now, this will push you over the cliff and you will fall into the abyss of life's down trodden.

As you can see, whatever is to happen is not going to be good for those of you that save **god/notes** to hedge your bets on the future. I believe the worst place you can have your money is in money.

The financial crisis of 2012 - 2013 in a small country called Cyprus, saw this government impose a small fee of 40% on all uninsured deposits held there in their country. And no other government in the world said a word,,, that is a word anyone could hear. I think they all just smiled,,, "wow, free money. See we don't need a budget."

October 9, 2014, an Executive Order from the President of the United States regarding authorizing the implementation of certain sanctions,,, was signed. These sanctions were designed to freeze all bank accounts and stop related financial transactions of a "sanctioned person" within America. Without a court order one man can take it all. If you are declared a "sanctioned person", everything you have can be taken from you without a trial and without being found guilty of anything.

This is not America where we have due process of law, but is starting to resemble a dictatorship under some type of....

Martial Law.

U.S.A. Camps

Global Financial Super Heating

Chapter Three

Dominoes

What will unfold?

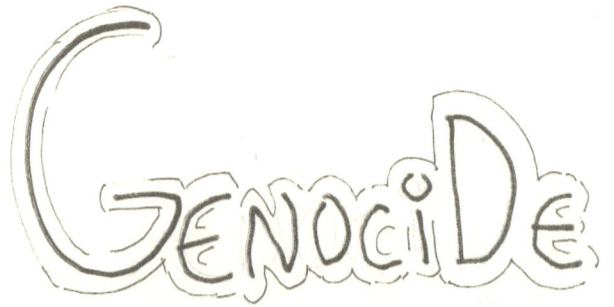

The Solution

House of Cards

The unraveling of the American economy will hit us hard in this country and we will see a depression as bad as the one in the 1930s or worse, because America will pull down the rest of the world as well. America, sometimes known as the policemen of the world and the most disabling country in the world will have to come home, for no one will take our bum checks anymore.

In God We Trust, was stamped on the first American coin in 1864, when we were at war with ourselves over states rights to govern themselves. Then during the cold war in 1957 it, **God**, was added to paper money because the **notes** were coming. I believe the first time this was done was to create a sense of stability and hold the country together using God. Any god will do as was done with the first green backs eye on top of the pyramid on the back of our dollar is meant to do. This eye reportedly is linked to Lucifer or the god of Qabbalah and some can work out magic from the stones and letters to mean 666. All links to the Christians and their religious undermining ignorant ways to control the masses.

However the second time God was added, (to our paper money), was not to hold us together but I believe driven by greed of those behind the one party system governing this country today, the super rich.

J.F.K.

John F. Kennedy, the first Roman Catholic president, wanted to end the Vietnam War and bring American solders home. But because he was closing it down (the war machine), he paid for his actions with his life. But was it the war mongers selling their goods or was it a higher order that came from the Vatican, for they could not spread the word of their god in Vietnam if John F. Kennedy was successful?

It is believed by many that on November 22, 1963 John F. Kennedy was murdered by the men who would take over this country, in a coup (not caring who knew) and then in bungling fashion cover it up. Their power so great to this day, and they still control the Dis-information Department of the federal government, as it turns out lie after lie to cover the trail of misinformation produced in the past. Making it all fit.

Global Financial Super Heating

The president's limousine was repaired within days after the shooting, as I understand, covering up any evidence of bullet holes and no one to my knowledge that did these repairs ever came forward to tell of the type of repairs that were done (number of bullet holes repaired).

One report that has come out is a bullet hole in the windshield of the JFK Limousine that 6 witnesses saw. But the one story of a man shot in the face by a stray fragment that had ricocheted off the curb in front of him is the hardest to cover up. They removed the hunk of curb and I think it may be gone for good but, James Tague carried the scar and the story until his death.

Reportedly Kennedy was killed with three bullets and they stuck to that story for years making all the evidence fit. Because Mr. Tague did not fit their story, he was never widely reported on,,, if at all. The thing is the bullets that killed JFK reportedly were all brass jacketed and the one fragment that hit Mr. Tague was all lead.

PBS the Public Broadcasting Service (government) did two in-depth _**stories**_ on the Kennedy murder; and in the first there were **three** bullets, not **four** or five or six. It would have been funny if it were not so sad as to how they were covering the whole thing up once more. Like how a bullet coming in the back of Mr. Kennedys head made a large chunk of his skull race across the trunk of the limousine with Mrs. Kennedy retrieving it.

Global Financial Super Heating

But the last PBS *story* was more in your face, *"we will make up anything we want and shove it down the people's throat and you will just swallow it"* than the one before. Seems since the last airing of their in-depth reporting, they have surmised there were only **two** bullets. Yes I said 2,,, we are now down to just 2 and I think at this rate by the time the real information comes out, if ever, the government will report there were no bullets at all and Kennedy died of old age.

I lost a lot of friends in that Christian crusade through Vietnam and some came home with holes in their bodies, missing limbs and all were screwed up in the head from the swamp war that we could not win. They would tell me, "Take a hill and give it back,,, it was insane." Many believe that war was started to spread Christian values, by any means right after WWII, to appease both the war mongers and the good Christian. Over 50,000 Americans died,,, for what,,, bombs and these Christian gods. And look at what those good Christians did to those Vietnamese people. How can they (the good Christians) look us in the face and pretend they do good work? As I understand after WWII France wanted its **colonial** power back over Vietnam and they moved into that country in 1946. The war mongers followed with the Christians at their side arm in arm and the Christian crusades were on to stop the new boogie man **communism**.

Kent State

When a government will openly kill its own people we have reached a new low. May 4, 1970 was a real shocker for me. I will never forget the day this government turned on Americans and opened fire, killing Jeffry Miller at Kent State, an unarmed young American and three others for a total of 4. *Yes I said 4 unarmed Americans.*

No one was ever prosecuted for the 4 murders and we know who did it. Eight guardsmen were indicted and they all pled **self-defense**. *Think of that, self-defense, from what?* This claim was accepted by the criminal justice system and the charges were dismissed. *Let's see now,,, four unarmed college kids,,, were such a threat that they had to kill them to save their lives and they got away with it.*

I believe the Christian leaders knew what they were doing and this non-prosecuting action sent a message to all the citizens of America, *"step out of line and we will kill you."* Protest slowed after that and we all stepped in line fearing the power behind the pretense of this military government. The power that could circumvent its laws and justice for all, seemed to grow greater and greater with each passing year. Is this why no banksters ever went to jail? The real power and Christians can circumvent the laws as they see fit and others are paid to look the other way. The federal government (George W. Bush) allegedly told each state **not** to prosecute the banksters,,, they (the federal government) would do it and they did nothing protecting their Christian and Jewish friends at the top of these banks.

I still see Jeffery Miller's body lying in the street with Mary Ann Vecchio kneeling next to him.

The more Christians step into power the more we all can see double standards like war crimes. The killing of innocent men women and children in other countries seemed to start to become more common place and acceptable over the years and from Christian president to Christian president, *"just part of doing the business of war as they spread their God Christian values,"* such as they are.

What power they have over this country and the world is mind numbing. The International Court of Justice is the primary judicial branch of the United Nations. In 1986 the United States **withdrew** from their jurisdiction, after they ruled in the Nicaragua Governments favor, that the American government **did covertly engage in war**.

A Christian president reportedly supported the Contras (right-wing Christian) rebellion against the Nicaraguan government and did engage in Mining their harbors.

Apparently if the Christians don't like your rulings, (world law) they are just not going to play in that game. The president at this time was Ronald Reagan, a Presbyterian (baptized as, Disciples of

Christ) another Christian doing God's work. When you put them in power this is what you get!

Tiananmen Square

On June 4, 1989 the Chinese apparently used a play from the Christian-American game book of life and killed its own people protesting in the streets (The Tiananmen Square Massacre or sometimes called the June 4 Massacre). Like America they controlled their people and I would bet that you would have to go to China to hear about the American Christian government that killed its own people,,, at Kent State.

I still see 'Tank Man' standing in front of the Chinese tank stopping it in the street. No one knows who Tank Man is to this day. It was clear to me he was just a passerby going home because he is holding bags of what look like food. One would not bring bags with you to a protest.

Separation

Laws are made to be broken as one religion slowly takes over a country. My fear is ISIS or Al Qaeda will be next. Covertly the Christians have circumvented the **Separation of Church and State** portion of our Constitution; and this religious cancer grows deeper into what is left of this government. Quietly, in May of this year (2014), the Supreme Court ruled in the favor of government meetings, open to the public, paid for with all our tax dollars, could start with a Christian prayer. A cult called Christianity that openly discriminates against women and homosexuality, will now dictate to the rest of us what they require in their **Morality Clause**. Another name for this could be **Witch Hunt**.

As of June 27th of this year (2014) the Christian Supreme Court ruled once again in the favor of a Christian law, and against pro-choice. They used the first amendment stating the Christians had the right to harass women in the public street, pushing their Christian God onto them. But that is a two-edged sword that can cut both ways. Will ISIS and Al Qaeda be next?

Will we become like Russia and will there be new laws against homosexuals? In some Christian led countries today, they now drag the gay people out into the street and kill them. In Russia (under Vladimir Putin, a Russian Orthodox or Christian) they (gays) can get a 30 prison sentence because they are gay. What will be next? Will it become mandated like in the Roman days, you will be a Christian or we will kill you? (Roman Christians killed Pagans and other non-Christians)

This year Russia has invaded the country of Ukraine taking over parts of their country **because they can** and claiming it as theirs. The interesting part is the part of Ukraine that is being destroyed looks to be Muslim. If I am reading the religious

Global Financial Super Heating

maps of that country right,,, this starts to look like another genocide where Christians are killing Muslims for their land,,, as we all sit back and say nothing.

Listen closely and you can hear the little Christian drummer boy tapping out his song, **onward Christian soldier***, as we all march backwards in time,,, into the dark ages.*

Will Al Qaeda and ISIS dance in the streets for they brought down the great Christian beast onto all the people? Showing the entire world, what those Christians truly are and with them (the Christians) the remaining life blood, the American dollar, will spill onto the dirt. This Christian-led government seems to have had one goal and that has been to kill as many Muslims as they could while spreading the word of their good Christian Gods. Can you have any question as to why Al Qaeda and ISIS are fighting back so hard and winning? They are defending their land, their people and their religion, taken by the Christians over the last thousand years.

It looks like **Christian Colonialism Wars** will end for America as we no longer can pay for them with borrowed money. Like the Germans did in WW1, no one will want to take the Christian downward spiraling American dollar or **god/note**.

Global Financial Super Heating

Businesses will close because they can't pay for goods and sell them for a profit to pay their bills. Unemployment will hit new record highs like this country has never seen before; and all the states that have run up record debts to pay for this last round of federally mandated unemployment extensions, will finally go belly up.

This federal unemployment extension mandate, is one more entitlement paid for with loans to the states by the federal government that borrows and prints the money. This debt is crushing to each state and now the federal government requires their borrowed money back and they want interest on the mafia forced loaned money. In Florida today, the state is going after the only remaining running businesses that have survived the depression of 2007. Their plan is to put the weight of this debt on the only ones left standing. Each surviving Florida business is to pay an additional amount of tax on each employee they have to pay the **interest** of this federally mandated unemployment extension or what I call, the 'make the Christian president feel good' law.

The federal government's policy of spend, spend, spend, will end, end, end. We will no longer be bailing out other countries with money we borrow from other countries. Other countries will not lend to us, so America can bail out the world trying to buy friends or pay for the endless Christian colonial war machine's bills. The price we will pay for spreading Christian values, or lack thereof, is coming and will be coming hard as in the 70s when we all paid the price of Jewish/Christian colonialism in Israel. Once more we all will pay the price for this god and the ones it chooses to battle with.

The bankruptcy courts will be overwhelmed with applications and the backup could take decades because the federal court system will have no money to pay for them.

The **austerity** requirements by other governments (living within our budget) will hit hard because other better run governments, like atheist communist China, (or the devil) will require us to take cuts in our budget before they will buy our bonds (loan us money) so we can pay our bills (interest on the money we have borrowed).

Did you know some states **record** **loans** as revenue? Can you imagine you get a loan from the bank and put it in the states checking account as spending money never to have to be paid back. Free money!!! Reminds me of my ex-wife, anything to look good and feel good deceiving the people as many good religions seem to do best.

The heat will be turned on in the financial markets of the world, as the enemies of America do everything they can to finish bringing down this Christian governed country. ISIS, Al Qaeda, Muslims, Russia, China, Saudi Arabia and everyone else that those good Christians have killed, lied to, stepped on, or stabbed in the back (while spreading the word of this the only religion to be permitted on the earth) will be coming at us from every direction.

So many lies, so many wrongs committed in the name of these prehistoric Christian Gods and at their own peril, these other countries will lose money if it brings down the beast,,, Christian America. Others will pick up the swords America can no longer carry and the killing will continue and the Jews, Christians and Muslims will not stop until their god and only their god rules. If there were an old man in the sky looking down on earth, what would he think of man and the things man does in his, (gods) name? If I were god I would disown them all.

The dark ages are coming at us very fast as our eyes are on the governments' diversions. How and when it all unfolds is not clear. As to which domino will be the first to fall or will history point to the one that has already fallen?

Reportedly this year governor Chris Christie, a Roman Catholic, apologized for referring to Jews as "**occupied territories**". I know he apologized because he offended the money god people, by referring to Jews as occupied territories. Did he say this because it is true or because of **Jewish Deicide?** (That is a belief that places the responsibility of Jesus Christ death on the Jews.)

Reportedly this year Governor Bill Haslam a Presbyterian (Christ God people) from Tennessee has signed a bill that makes it mandatory to use the electric chair to kill people in his state. Seems thou shall not kill,,, does not apply to Presbyterian or convicts, as we look to religious leaders for guidance.

The Christians must be dancing in the streets as they gain power over all of us in Louisiana. It was reported a bill could force three of the five abortion clinics in that state to close. Are these second class female citizens, stepping out of Christian line, when they want to control their own bodies? Are they joined by those that wish to rise up in the Mormon Church like Kate Kelly reportedly tried and was found guilty of apostasy by what I understand to be an all male Christian tribunal? Why do women think they have rights in any religion? Must be part of gods plains.

One of the most sickening events of the year comes from Seattle where this year it was reported the Catholic archdiocese is to pay twelve million god dollars to settle sex abuse claims. A disturbing part of this is, it will cost them **nothing** out of pocket for the church has **INSURANCE**. I am not making this up, the archdiocese has insurance to cover such things. Can you imagine such a policy and the conversation? *"Yes,,, I can see the need to insure against people getting upset because we in the church will have sex with little boys,,, so sign me up."*

And we all sit back,,, say and do nothing. Well what can we do? Go after the ones that covered it up!!! Settled out of court or not,,, they broke the law!!! Why are they all not in jail?

The following cartoon is based on a news report this year of a Christian soup kitchen in South Carolina that would not take help from an atheist organization that only wanted to help feed the poor and was horribly rebuffed.

I just don't get it!

Where is the Christian love they always speak of?

Get out atheist,,, we know what you are!!!

A soup kitchen in South Carolina

William J. Ryan 2014 copyright © #077

Global Financial Super Heating

Chapter Four

Global Shading

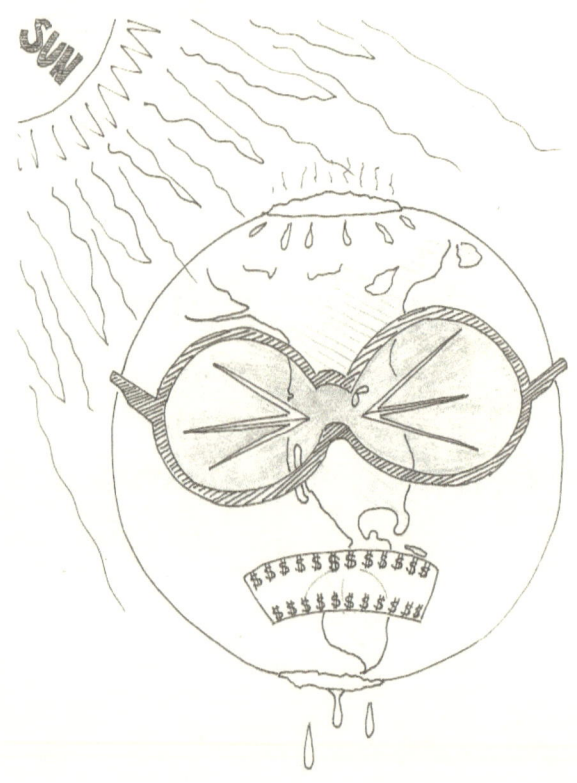

Time's up
Game over

Global Shading

Not many are talking about this because the powers don't want us underlings (keep the masses ignorant so they can be controlled) and the Goyim to panic over the knowledge, that our past 100 years of endless gluttonies (or the industrial years) have taken a total on this planet much worse than most know. When the effect of our endless spending and Christian Colonialism, as well as other religions, starts to wind down, and it will happen, people will start to understand the full effects of wasted resources and that climate change is real and here now. Not 100 years away or 50 years or 25 years but here right now!

We all will be doing our best to keep the home fires going and cutting back as paper money or **gods/notes** drop through the floor where they belong. Your plans to see the world before you die as part of your bucket list will have to be done at home looking at pictures in old magazines. Your home may be your car if you can hide it from the bank, which will be hiding from the federal government and all the foreign investors. All the people across the globe that the Christians have been persecuting in **American interest,** will rise up and seek out revenge for all the Christian destructive, heartless theft of their resources, destruction of their land, and the murdering of their people in gods name.

Christian Americans are a funny lot, for they say they invade a country to help, however,,, *if they don't have resources (oil) that meet American interests, (like Tibet) Christians don't care if people are destroyed. Their women suffer sterilization while the land becomes a dumping ground and China commits genocide.* Tibet only meets a small portion of the requirement for intervention. It's too bad they don't have wealth, oil or Christians so America would help them. They just don't meet the requirements of the BIG 3.

All types of religious revenge will began across the globe, for the Christians have **supplied** our enemies with all manner of weapons to come back and kill Americans.

And that is when it will start

If you're as old as I am and you grew up in the 50s and 60s you will remember how blue the sky used to be and how clean the air was. When the sun would set behind the tree line there was no orange sky, just dimming bright white light that lasted for an hour after the sun set until the sky filled with bright stars.

Now the pollutions in the air turn the sun a dim dirty orange as the light quickly disappears before it sets. But since the 50s the skies have filled with a new pollution that no one talks about. Now I am not talking about the radioactive waste leaking into the drinking water aquifers now evaporating into the air, no-no, nor is this about Fukushima. I am talking about the **contrails from the jumbo jets** that fly the rich and the super rich all over the planet so they can have fun, while the rest of us pay the true price.

The air lines have been supported by the federal government from an early time and still to this day we all pay to fly empty planes to empty airports in some states just to keep them open. Federal dollars help to keep the price of a ticket well below the true cost, encouraging people to fly and pollute the skies.

They use up all our air **because they can**, they are the rich. The skies are full of endless streams of the jet people going someplace using up all the clean air. But we all have been enjoying a side effect of the rich traveling the globe for fun and profit and that is *Global Shading*.

Contrails or vapor trails are long thin artificial clouds that sometimes form from aircrafts very high in the air. Small bits of pollution coming from the jet engines traversing the globe stay in the upper altitudes 8,000 to 36,000 ft. As I understand the particles are too small to gather moisture and fall back to the earth as rain, so they stay up there floating about. Days later some of these small bits travel back to earth joining the rest of the air pollution closer to the ground.

The benefits are that while they are in the upper atmosphere, these contrails **reflect** the sun's rays and help keep the earth's temperature lower. Or just keep it from rising at a faster rate than it would **without** the reflective contrails. The earth is kept cooler by this pollution. Without these contrails we would have seen the effects of global warming hit us hard a long time ago.

The following chart was created only to help show the **death path** we are on regarding Carbon Dioxide (burning of fossil fuels) and the future that lies before us all,,, if we do nothing and say nothing.

Global Financial Super Heating

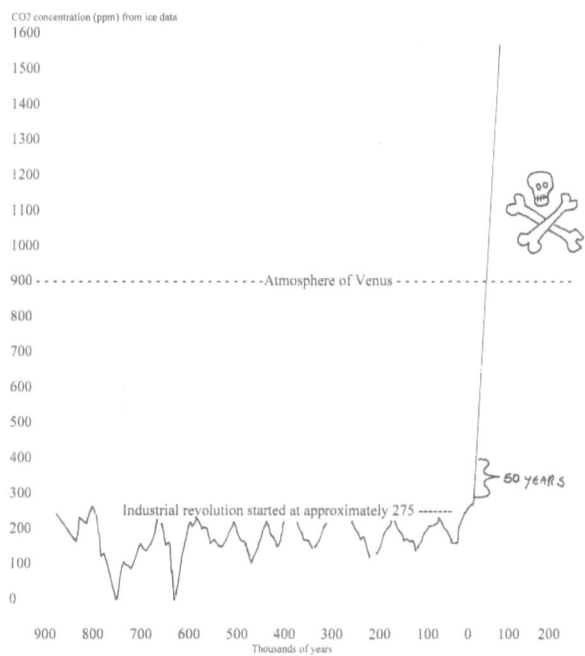

Carbon Dioxide Atmospheric Chart
An accumulation of mutable studies assembled in approximate values to show only future values.

CO2 concentration (ppm) from ice data

Industrial revolution started at approximately 275 ------

------------------------Atmosphere of Venus-------------------

50 YEARS

Thousands of years

William J. Ryan ©2014 #038

Death Path

Global Financial Super Heating

Atmospheric charts show the earth's peaks and valleys of CO_2 over the past 900 thousand years to be between 100 and 200 parts per million (ppm). This is my quick estimate as an average over time, however in the past 900 thousand years the CO_2 count has climbed at or near 300 ppm. But today it is climbing **straight up** since the industrial revolution and in 1970 was reported to be about 325 ppm. By 1995 it had reached 380 ppm (in just 25 years, a new uncharted dangerous and deadly territory) and I believe that growth factor will continue, unabated. The sustained high of 300 ppm may see palm trees on the north and south poles but a high of 600 ppm or 1200 ppm will see only death for all, if we do nothing.

Now these predictions of 600 ppm to 1200 ppm are my estimates and only reflect a continued growth in CO_2 production from man. At the worst (1200 ppm) what will life hold for all of us in the future? I just don't see one if we continue to do nothing.

Why do I think 1200 ppm is a real number? For the past 900 thousand years the CO_2 level has remained somewhat stable. But in just under 200 years we on this small planet have seen CO_2 levels grow from that normal level of 100 ppm to 200 ppm to levels well past the historical peak high of just under 300 ppm. Then in just 25 years is has shot up by 55 ppm and by some estimates the true number is at or over 400 ppm, making the growth in the past 45 years about 75 ppm. That is almost 1.7 ppm per year with no end or stopping point in sight. It is moving straight up,,, no end in sight if we do nothing!

This Global Shading theory was tested in recent time when all the jet-setters had to sit on their butts with the rest of us and look up to the empty sky. That time was September the day was the eleventh the year was 2001 the time was 8:50 and 9:03 as George W. Bush sat on his ass reading child's books to first graders in a class room in Sarasota, Florida. When told of the first plane, his look to some was of a man that knew it was coming,,, (no surprise) he just sat there and continued with the kids, as thousands of people died, in this 21 century Perl Harbor. Sometime after the second plane hit he was **pulled away** and then got on his plane and allegedly,,, ran for cover. Some place safe,,, from the danger,,, that seemed to be all around George,,, like the Devil or the Boogie Man for all Christians suffering from **Scrupulosity**.

The only two fighter jets available on the entire east coast of the United States were launched, but by then the four planes were back on American soil leaving much death and destruction. Many believe this was revenge for Christians killing Muslims all over the world.

It should be noted, for the next three days most air travel came to a halt and the skies were empty of planes. Reportedly the air temperature rose (if I remember it correctly) by 1.5 degrees across the globe within those three days,,, telling you what?

Some believe George (a born again Christian or convict Christianity) and his Christian henchmen (with preconceived, before 911, war plans to invade Iraq) went into hyper drive and he then invaded a country that had done nothing to us,,, in and for God's name. Their only crime (Iraq) was to have oil that bush wanted for his campaign contributors and one of the excuses was aluminum tubes lying on the ground. Later George was allegedly quoted as saying, "he (Saddam Hussein) tried to kill my daddy". But I believe America invaded that country, <u>which did nothing to us</u>, because that action of war meets the requirements of the **Big 3** (oil, money and god). Christians wanted to kill Muslims and what better way than to free them to kill themselves. Let my enemies kill my enemies.

This invasion is much like what Hitler did in WWII,,, when he invaded Europe,,, countries that had done nothing to him or the German soldiers that fought and killed all those people just defending themselves from the intruders on their land. Can there really be any wonder why **American** soldiers return home and kill themselves? For they must carry the same shame Hitler's men must have,,, **GOTT MIT UNS** "God with us", in this most recent Christian crusade. These brave freedom fighters are murdering invaders to many of the indigenous people. We don't openly talk about this but look hard at the facts and you may find the Christians are behind the murder of these people under the pretense of peace and love.

The war profiteers in 2001 could not wait to get their hands on all the money, as the Christian leaders turned in on ourselves, spying on all Americans, as the Germans did to their people in WWII. Reportedly the only building in Iraq our peace keeping freedom fighters protected was the **oil administration**. They let the rest go to hell before their eyes. Including, but not limited to, the water and sewer plants, the schools, hospitals, air ports, roads, bridges, churches, temples and museums. These acts, or lack of acting, ended up throwing these poor people in this country into the dark ages as over one hundred thousand women, children and innocent men were killed, all for oil, war suppliers, and of course,,, God's sake. These are the big three: **Oil, Money/War Profiteers, and Spreading God's Word**.

Saddam Hussein did his best to keep peace in his country with a firm hand and the streets were safe. Up to this time Saddam protected his people from the Al Qaeda's religious wackos. But now, like another religious cancer, that we help bring into Iraq, Christian America gives money to Pakistan and they give it to Al Qaeda. Al Qaeda buys war supplies to fight off the Christian murdering invaders and the war is escalated justifying the presents of the **BIG 3**. Al Qaeda is stronger now than before, and with American war supplies, ISIS, that is even more backwards in its religious intolerance than Al Qaeda and Christians, seems to be taking over Iraq. Could this be all part of the Christian plan? Have we seen this movie before? Are the war mongers using Christians to destabilize a Muslim country so they (Muslims) will rise up and defend themselves and their land and be labeled terrorists so the Christians can justify invading their country and indiscriminately killing them (Muslim) all? From my vantage point on the outside it looks like Christians from all countries have been killing Muslims and Jews for a very long time and still are.

One story from this time has always stuck in my mind and that is the fiftieth attempt (50th) on Saddam Hussein's life. Reportedly one of our paid Iraq spies pointed to a house where Saddam Hussein was reportedly staying. Now 49 times before this Christian led military was told wrongly of Saddam Hussein's location and innocent people died. This last time was to be no different. That day the United States of America's bombs were dropped on a home killing a woman and her two small girls. The father was at work, like good fathers should be, when his family was killed by our Christian soldiers. Yet no one paid a price, *other than the person or persons that pressed the buttons or pulled the trigger that killed so many innocent people. They must live with what they did and try to find peace in the words "I was just following orders."* (War crimes, Nuremberg Trial, 1947)

Reportedly after that day the father returned home and in his grief he stated he only wanted to kill Americans. Who could blame him? It was then for the first time I could see a little better what was going on. I could understand his grief and I thought, how I would feel, if that happened to me.

Could it be true, George is a Christian and beyond the oil could he be spreading the power of his God to the rest of the world? If one looks closely, this Christian American government is killing Muslims and, for the most part, only Muslims, all over the world. Could this be the reason why Muslims are trying to kill us back? I have heard it said, "America is the most destabilizing country in the world" and I believe this is right and it started when God was permitted to entered this government as part of the **BIG 3's** takeover,,, **Marshall Law**,,, total control.

It was after seeing that man's grief over the loss of his home and family, murdered by the Christians and his vowing to only want to kill Americans that I could understand. I could put myself in his place and I too, facing such a loss, would grab a gun and help kill the **invaders** of my country. My enemy that heartlessly killed my family (as collateral damage) while trying to kill one man **without even knowing if he was actually there**. Could they not have found another way or check first? Are these people's lives that valueless just because they are Muslim? I just don't understand and I don't think I ever will.

The plan of Al Qaeda was to bring down the godless American government that we trusted to protect us,,, and from where I sit,,, looking forward,,, they did. We have been in a tailspin ever since their attack (not **The BIG 3**) and regardless of how much money this government prints and spends to keep the pretenses of this government afloat, we are at lightning speed steadily crashing.

Many theorize that Christian hands are on this American ship of state, as they drive it over the fiscal cliff, all in God's name, but is that the total truth? Some believe the Christian ideology brought down the Roman Empire, brought about no less than five crusades for God and money, they (followers of this ideology) started WWII, invaded Iraq and with the same reckless disregard for us all, they are about to bring down America. What is to come we can all lay at the feet of their imaginary gods, (Muslim, Judaism and Christianity) or are they being used? The state of the financial calamity that is to come is substantially the responsibility of religions and their gods,,, for they permit it to happen. They want war.

As this cancer called Christianity moves into our once free government, knocking down the wall of **Separation of Church and State** and grinding it into dust under our feet, turning it into a memory, not a fact, we all must learn to live in fear as this government legalizes the murdering of Americans without a trial or due process of law. Reportedly this is openly happening overseas. When will it happen in this country,,, or has it already? Kent state to name but one and remember they (the **BIG 3**) don't care if you know. As a mater in fact, it's better for them if you do know. Fear is a power tool of control and of war.

Are secret courts, secret prisons, black money, kidnapping people across the globe and taking them to countries for legal torture and the murdering of Americans without a trial, but a small part of the future we all must recognize as Christian? We are moving backwards in time under their domination. Would we do nothing if they were Al Qaeda or ISIS? To some they are the same,,, all religious terrorists.

But are the ills of the world truly to be laid at the feed of God and all religions? Is it their hand (religion) on the ship of state or ones that stand behind God using God's power over the masses? That would make God and all his followers just pawns in someone else's game.

But who would use God and religion for their own **financial** gains? From where I sit,,,

everyone.

Super Heating

So what does money have to do with global warming or heating? It has to do with the fact that the stage is set for **very fast** global warming that I call **Global Financial Super Heating**. We seem to be doing a lot of talking about global warming, as we do our best to use up every natural fossil fuel as fast as we can, so they (**The BIG 3**) can make as much money as possible.

The world has grown accustomed to the American dollar and it is good and used in every country. Oh wait,,, it's not so good anymore and its use is on the decline. We (America) have been warned to get our spending under control,,, but that is no fun,,, especially when there are so many Muslims and Jews to kill (Jewish Deicide). Besides the people on K Street in Washington need our tax and borrowed money for their business (American interest $$$$$) and if the politicians want to be reelected to their office, (keep their jobs) they take the money (bribes). So the endless spending keeps on going and will not stop until we are on our knees,,, broken by this Christian agenda,,, brought to you by **The BIG 3**.

This decline will continue as investors move away from the dollar. Large companies are moving their corporations overseas to avoid paying taxes and to distance themselves from what is to come,,, **the crash of the American dollar.**

Global Financial Super Heating

It will start slowly and most of us will not notice a thing. As of now, things are not getting better and no matter how hard we all work someone or something is there to take our money. We just can't get ahead.

As more and more countries back away from the American dollar it loses its power and strength and becomes less valuable. That will only mean the price of everything will go up or just take more of these paper **god/note** dollars to buy things and when food costs more and gasoline costs more we will continue to **spend less on** other things like **travel**.

In the future we will visit our families on the net or on the phone or like the old days, just write them a letter and so will business. Greater cost cutting will be part of the American life style as those on the brink of collapse will fall into the financial abyss that is to come.

Then at some point the government may make an adjustment (a quick fix). It will, or may, downgrade the value of the U.S. dollar, screwing people all over the world out of money; or it will just not pay on its debt, screwing people all over the world out of their money; or it will print more money screwing people all over the world. The outcome is the same. If you have your money in money you most likely will lose money and if you have your money in the shark market you are D.O.O.M.ed. D.O.O.M. stands for **Devaluing Of Our Money**.

Global Financial Super Heating

This will have the effect of unraveling the fabric of this and other nations and most all commerce will slow, or come to an end, as we all try to adjust to the ever falling dollar's value. Like a snail we all will pull back into our shell and try to ride this out but the fall is going to be hard. Not days or weeks but more like over years the dollar will decline and as in Germany (after WW1) and other countries that have tried this quick fix (D.O.O.M. or the printing of unlimited currency or our trillion dollar coin) in the past,,, but failed,,, there is no stopping it quickly. Many believe the crash is coming soon and I believe these hard times will bring about **Super Heating** of the planet.

As I said before, everyone will pull back. Factories will shut down, people will stay home, drive less, and pollution over our cities will decline. Fewer people will get on planes, unable to afford the new higher (shrinking dollar) prices, to fly. Businesses that survive will not have the need to travel like they did in good times because the dollar is dropping so fast they stay in their offices. Everyone will cut back and that will cause a lot of business to crash.

Air lines no longer supported by this government will start bleeding red ink within months if not weeks and they too will crash (as the Concorde did, 1969 to 2003) unable to pay for fuel to get their planes home as they go belly up, stranding people all over the globe.

As there are less and less planes in the skies the upper atmosphere will start to clear and those beautiful bright blue skies will return with long bright sunsets. But what cost will these cleaner skies have on all of us and the planet where we live,,, with its damaged ozone and lower oxygen levels due to the reckless behavior of those greedy for **god/notes**?

Reportedly some claim the ozone in the earth's stratosphere has reduced fewer than 5% per year since the end of the 1970s. Other reports claim it has stopped reducing. That is just hard to believe that it has stopped completely. The hole and lack of its protections is allegedly responsible for increases in skin cancer and cataracts. As well as damage to plankton and plants as the UV exposure grows.

Without the protection of the jets con trails the earth's temperature will rise and rise fast. The one good thing we have going for us is reportedly the federal government of America uses 50% of all the oil used by this country. If this government were to come home and stop spending money all over the planet, enriching **The BIG 3**, we could cut our oil consumption and not need other countries' oil. But if they did those government contrails would be gone as well as private commercial planes.

It's going to get hot!

Global Financial Super Heating

Chapter Five

The Canary In The Coal Mine

150 years to put in to the air
"dont worry... we know what we are doing."

William J. Ryan 2014 copyright © #076

Global Financial Super Heating

We all see the signs but don't see what future warnings they point to. For you that may not know what the phrase *"canary in the coal mine"* means I will tell you. In the 1800s coal miners would take a canary (a small song bird) with them into the mines to detect explosive poison gas found in the rocks they were digging in. If the bird died they knew it was time to get out.

Such warnings are all around us if we would just take time to look and realize just how the cause and effect of our environment will overtake us. Primarily in the past 100 years we have been killing off creatures that we need, that share this planet with us, at an alarming rate.

Reportedly in the 1930s **a business** brought a frog from Africa to America because it had qualities that helped in the development of pregnancy tests. This is a good thing because it helped to slow down the numbers of new unwanted mouths to feed (much to the dismay of the Christians). The bad thing is allegedly those frogs brought with them a toxic fungus that disables the amphibian immune system called Batrachochytrium dendrobatidis and that fungus has started to cross the globe leaving dead frogs all across the United States and Mexico as well as other continents.

I can tell you I bought my property over ten years ago and each night there would be hundreds of frogs on it. Each time it rained they would be out there croaking and breeding and **eating bugs**. This year of 2014 I have seen no more than 20 frogs here this year. *That is a reduction of over 98% in my view.*

I have a friend that lives near the Florida swamps (his back yard), as close as one would want to live and I asked him if he noticed fewer frogs around his home and the question stunned him. He thought for a moment and said yes.

Because this fungus may have created so many dead frogs, the future is clear. Birds have no frogs to eat and feed their young. Snakes eat frogs and rodents. Frogs eat mosquito larva and some birds eat mosquitoes!!! If the mosquito population grows unchecked (uneaten), it will spread its diseases to the other mammals (like us). We need frogs or more life will die, diseases will spread and the bug population will grow.

Unchecked and unregulated by the decline in populations of birds and the amphibian species, all manner of insect populations will grow and this man-made disaster will cross the globe. It happened in China around 100 years ago when the black bird was declared a nuisance to all man (by their government), because it ate the seeds in the freshly planted farm fields and the government put a bounty on the small bird and they were hunted to near extinction. What followed were swarms of uneaten insects that had a devastating effect on the crops, and as a result people starved.

In the near future with the lack of predators, bugs, with their voracious appetite and their new resistances to insecticides, will eat every living thing they can. I'll bet there will not be a green leaf left standing when they are done. And there is no fixing this man made annual event. The skies will darken with their locust like waves creating new sights for us all in the form of Bug-nados.

As the world's ground temperature climbs permitting insect populations to spread ever further and even faster, diseases will head north towards us. Reportedly, **malaria** is now in southern Mexico where these frog populations have all but disappeared.

Fire ants, crazy ants, killer bees, the recluse spider and vampire bats just to name a few southern tropical forms of life have worked their way north into the United States. More will come as the planet gets warmer and warmer, so we all need to just get used to it.

It only makes sense that infectious diseases from mosquitoes are the next thing to be coming this way. As we become a third world Christian nation, living in the dark ages.

Global Financial Super Heating

1. Dengue fever
2. Malaria
3. Rift Valley Fever
4. Yellow fever
5. Zaire ebolavirus
6. Ebola

These are but a few diseases that could be heading our way very soon and there will be no stopping it. Someone will carry it up here, most likely on a train or boxed in our food or it will come on the wind,,, but it will come.

It should be noted that many believe the federal government welcomed with open arms Ebola, because they believed they could control it and after spending all that money building facilities to do such a thing,,, they needed to test them. But could there be another reason?

The first one (Ebola idiot) brought back to this country was a Christian and taken to a Christian hospital,,, risking all Americans without a care,,, for they are doing God's work and are above the law and only concerned with saving a Christian. But who let them in and why?

Fungi

I try to envision every possible type of ailment that will cross our paths and fungus is one that keeps popping up in my mind. To grow a good healthy batch of fungus some need a dark moist environment for best results.

Mammals have such a place and as air breathing creatures we suck in all manner of foreign particles that must be removed from the body. Our lungs could be a host to a strain of fungus like the one killing all the frogs.

Today there are a large variety of fungi that grow on our skin so why not our lungs. One cough and it is airborne, aiding the reproduction of its life cycle. Only thing is this fungus will most likely kill the host for how does one put anti-fungus cream on the tissue of one's lung?

Pneumonia is such an inflammatory illness that is the result of a virus, bacteria, fungus, or spores of some type could be the next killer. However it comes, I see this as one of the big killers that is to come,,, with the heat.

Global Financial Super Heating

Chapter Six

Water

Global Financial Super Heating

As everything warms from the absence of the pollution of our air that the wealthy and the super rich usually do with their jumbo jets every day, the **Global Financial Super Heating** will start to hit high gear. As I try to look forward in time I can see the weather changing all across the planet depending on the prevailing winds.

I remember hearing of a small community in South America on the Pacific Ocean side that suffered from changes in the winds that blew consistently from the ocean. As the winds pass over the water it creates waves but this wind was so strong it raised the water level and flooded the community for four years. When the winds changed course the water subsided and the people could return home. That was wind induced flooding that lasted for years.

As the planet continues to warm these winds will create new and stronger weather patterns across the globe and one year those winds will bring rain and the next dry heat and sun. For us Americans, I can see the drought that has all Californians in its grip, will only take a greater hold. Rivers, lakes, and streams will disappear as they have been, if we only will look. When you cut down all the trees, there is nothing to hold back the water, nothing to keep the earth from drying out and no place for other plants and animals to live,,, when the trees are all gone.

This large food producer (California) will dry up and only help accelerate the devaluing of money, by driving up the price of our food. To most of us who follow money, know that California is the great welfare state and relies heavily on the rest of our borrowed tax dollars to keep it in business. Three of its cities come to mind that have filed bankruptcy in the recent past few years and more will follow. As the water goes,,, so goes the tax money **revenue** for that state.

Their drought will only worsen as the state gets hotter and hotter. The snow California relies on will no longer be there to take care of these people. The highways will look like Detroit Michigan in the 70s when GM closed all those plants and our jobs moved far to the south with our middle class dollars.

The states of Wyoming, South Dakota, Nebraska, Colorado, Kansas, New Mexico, Oklahoma and Texas sit on the Ogallala Aquifer and it is reportedly **<u>50% gone</u>** in just over 30 years.

We have gone from full of water 100 years ago to finding it and starting to suck it out to feed small farms, then cities in the desert, to using it to produce food by spraying it on the ground like it had no value and there was no end to its supply. A few get rich (the American dream) while the rest of us pay the price,,,

no water!!!

It is easy to see that at this present rate of consumption this aquifer will mostly be gone by 2025 (10 years). The food it produces will also be gone and this too will be running up the price of food even higher as the **god/note** dollar continues to drop in perceived value.

The California Aqueduct system will be one of the first to dry up and then the eight states on the Ogallala Aquifer will most likely be next. If this cuts the American food supply by only 25% what will it do to the price of food? The cost of food in some countries today is the family's greatest expense. So try to wrap your head around the fact that in as little as 10 years from now food to feed your family could cost more than your house, your car, and your insurance, if you still own any of those things.

These people will leave their drought ridden communities in droves for places with water, taking with them whatever they can carry. With whatever money they have they will buy your home and drink your water. But where will you go to find water?

The new Blue Gold.

The global temperature will rise in these first few years of crashing god/notes by only a few degrees, (1 to 10) but it will bring surface temperatures at your home from a normal summer time high for us here in Florida of 96 degrees (our normal highest temperatures) to a high of 100 to 105 degrees as a norm. Not too bad you say, but the days will start hotter and the cool down will not be as quick for the land is baked from the heat. But we in Florida will most likely have our afternoon clouds and rains bringing us cooler temperatures and **Blue Gold**.

The surface water across the southern region of America (north of Florida) will be sucked away by the burning sun. I can envision the deserts in California and Arizona will cross the Mississippi river and head for Washington DC, where it belongs at the feet of this Christian mafia capital.

The Mississippi almost dried up in the year of 2013 where barges could barely make it up this new narrow stream that was once a wide mighty river. And what do you think will happen when it gets hotter?

When the air is that much hotter and dryer, people will be sucking the water out of rivers to water their gardens for food and the poor people downstream will do without. People in the cities of Baton Rouge and New Orleans will have to find a way to drink salt water as the states above them take their fill and they will become just more on the list that will have no water to drink as the gulf of Mexico laps at their door steps, higher and higher with the passing of every day, due to the melting of the north and south poles - two of the biggest air conditioners of the planet.

At some point the military will have to come home and protect our borders from the mass migration of people fleeing the south as their water runs out. We will no longer have the money to process these people and put them on a plane to send them back home. We will just erect guard towers and warn the hopeful that wish to come to America illegally; we will shoot on sight any one crossing that border. And that will end that. Our new immigration law will be,

"get out or we will kill you!!!"

There may be another plan underfoot and going on right in front of our eyes if only we will take the time to look. But you must stop and look at the bigger picture going on all around you. If one will apply the theory of **The Big 3** to all events going on around the world and within the United States, things will become clearer.

This government has anticipated the lack of water in the Colorado River and has erected a new lower tower to suck in water to run the Hoover dam. The two old towers once under water now stick out like pyramids of a lost ghost nation of people long ago gone. In the future, will we stare at it in wonderment?

"Oh yes, those towers were built by the plastic people (modern man). You only have to scrape the earth with your foot to unearth some part of their plastic destructive lives."

Alzheimer's and algae

Reportedly there is a link between blue-green algae and ALS and Alzheimer's disease. Where the human pollution has grown, blue - green alga is invading their water resources primarily due to inadequate treated wastewater creating high concentrations of plant nutrients. Toxins are a byproduct of blue-green algae and produce BMAA or beta-methyl-amino-alanine.

This toxin is crossing the globe and in countries unable to afford to process water properly, it is becoming highly concentrated in their water. It is my understanding that fish eat algae and people eat fish. If the algae fish eat is full of toxins that are stored in their fat and muscle we are eating high concentrates of this toxin. Fish don't live long lives so the toxins do not bother them, but we do and it appears to be stored in fat or end up in our brains and spinal cord tissues.

Soy-lent-green?

Spirulina reportedly is a cyanobacteria bacteria that can be eaten by humans and allegedly is made of blue-green algae,,, the safe kind I would hope. Is this to become the new food source and will we all just take our chances with the toxins that may or may not be in this new food? Reportedly there are concerns over even low levels of microcystins being consumed by humans and have showed liver and kidney damage as well as cancer over long term.

Heavy Metals

A byproduct of fossil fuel such as the burning of coal, natural gas and petroleum produces toxic metals that are now found everywhere on earth. We human beings as I understand require some heavy metals like cobalt, copper, manganese, Zink and iron to survive. The productions of these manmade toxic heavy metals are in the air we breathe and the water we drink and the food we eat. It is only logical that diseases will accrue from this and the only safe place I can think to hide, is away from cities and big manufacturing plants.

Hydraulic Fracturing

America does not need Al Qaeda or ISIS to come here and kill us,,, we have our very own religious wacko Christian led government to fulfill their dream of a toxin poisoned land filled with death and destruction, all for that paper **god/note** money that Christians and **The BIG 3** seem to value so much.

As I understand hydraulic fracturing is when criminal organizations **buy** the **Christian politicians** or poli-Christians that are for sale in Washington and have laws passed that they can pump <u>unregulated toxic chemicals</u> into the ground with no regard for the well-being of the people above that must drink the water that is poisoned by these,,, for profit corporations.

Side note: to show how misleading broadcast television is,,, a so called weekly news magazine reported this year 2014, these for profit hydraulic fracturing corporations were only pumping **<u>water</u>** *into the earth to release the wanted gas.* **Water,,, not toxic chemicals!!!** *An out and out lie!!! I wonder how much he was paid to say that and is he a Christian?*

Long after the gas is removed and the **god/note** money is earned and spent, these people that did this will be long gone and I'll bet these toxins will be in the drinking water for thousands of years. Every time there is an earth quake this time bomb of death will ooze up from below and wipe the land clean of every living thing that needs water to live.

Thanks Christians
Thanks BIG 3

Global Financial Super Heating

Chapter Seven

Salton City

Combination of Lake Cahuilla (Salton Sea) – approximately 250ft below sea level and Death Valley – approximately 500ft below sea level, before Mother Nature does it for us.

It is going to happen!

William J. Ryan ©2014 #053

Global Financial Super Heating

There is a relatively new small city in the middle of Southern California called Salton City. It is in the Colorado Desert of Imperial and Riverside counties. Its population is at or near 300 and it is an accident. Reportedly back in the 1905 heavy rains flooded this low and dry land creating a lake and people started to move there in the 50s with dreams of a good life and to make money developing the land. Yes, the almighty **god/note** strikes again.

But that one time flash of flood rain water was not to happen twice, at least not in that same magnitude and, allegedly, new man made dams prevent such things from occurring. They now are bypassed by any runoff and big rich cities suck up all the water they once relied on to keep this new lake full. So over the years this new lake, full of fish, has slowly been shrinking in size and depth as it is evaporating in the relentless desert sun and there are massive fish die-offs. If left to the environment and man this will dry up and the man made toxins from the farms runoff to the north will be swept on the wind and fill the air with all manner of new death.

So why talk about it?

In the future, after the **Global Financial Super Heating** has changed weather patterns and helped to expand the desert region of this area, water or the new **Blue Gold** will be very rare. It was hard to come by before in California, as water was moved to this region by large pipes and aqueducts, but I believe that water they now rely on also will disappear. This system brought badly needed water over the mountains to this dry land and this system is known as the California Aqueduct System.

When this source of water is gone, dried up or taken by others (farmers), the pipes will sit empty. No longer able to supply Southern California with endless free water to pour on the ground to make money supplying food for the rest of us, those pipes could find a better use. Extend those pipes to the sea and reverse the flow. Now it may not be practical to use those same pipes but you get the idea.

The oceans will have been picked clean by the big processing ships (of the rich countries like America and Japan) that make our fast food industries rich by making square fish sandwiches and those ships will be sitting idle.

With no fish in the seas, great plumes of uneaten dead decaying bacteria will create gases that will rise to the top and fill the air with new pollutants, as all nations search for another food source.

Could Algae or microscopic unicellular organisms become our new food source? A type of green sandwiches on the menu, offered at a low price from the fast food restaurant nearest you,,, any color and flavor you like.

However if you are turned off by that prospect then where do we find a controlled source of unlimited water that we can control 100% and use as a new source to grow food to feed a hungry nation? We have two, the Salton Sink and Death Valley.

Now remember water or **Blue Gold** will be gone for the most part in this area, as well as most of the people, and we will need food for the people that are left in this nation as it bakes in the sun. This is no small undertaking and will require a lot of engineering to complete. But we as a nation will require a food source that can be controlled and protected from outsiders and polluters.

As I see it there are two ways to accomplish this. **One,** is to do it ourselves and control it completely. Or **two**, we can sit back and wait for Mother Nature to do her thing. But it will happen someday. That someday maybe tomorrow, with the next big quake or 100,000 years from now, but it will happen on its own and we need the food now. We need to make plans now,,, for we don't have centuries or even decades to think about this.

We are long overdue for the big earth quake in southern California along the San Andreas Fault that strikes every 125 years or so and when it hits it will be the end for most people living there. That or the lack of water will have people leaving in droves. But the side effect could be that new fissures will open up and the people of Salton City will finally receive the water they have long been praying for. You know that God thing for them, will be coming true.

It could come as a trickle at first through the new cracks in the walls of the mountain ranges to the west of Salton. Or after the quake and with rising sea water it could come from the Gulf of California and cross through the city of Yuma.

In Japan, after the 2011 quake, they saw **cities drop five feet**. However it comes, over years the water will return. But reportedly Salton City sits 226 feet below sea level and the water will not stop at the banks of the current old shore line some 200 feet below sea level. It will just keep coming until the balance of water will level with the Pacific Ocean.

This could become a new salt water lake and the fish will be abundant as it will be fished to its limits. It also will become a new source of mosquito borne diseases. People can come to fish, but bring your own drinking water and bug repellent.

Another example of low land in the world is the Dead Sea also known as Salt Sea. It is a lake bordering Israel and Jordan (*or the center of Palestine, depending on what year Christian map you look at*) and it sits over 1,400 feet below sea level. On the side nearest the ocean, salt water seeps through the mountain ranges draining into this lake. Some day this lake (the Dead Sea) too, will become filled with salt water and full of fish (as I understand plate tectonics). The question is, do we as a people wait or do something now? They too maybe just one quake away from Mother Nature deciding for them but until then they wait for her.

The water or **Blue Gold** in this south western region of America will continue to disappear and so will the people as things get hotter and hotter. For no one can survive without water. If we continue to do nothing and permit our resources of clean drinking water to sink into the ground or pour into the sea, we will face new battles among our own people.

States that have water will start to see an influx of the needy and the greedy. Fresh water lakes that have not dried up will be under attack by droves of the thirsty. Each state that has water must face the question, *"How can **we** in **our** state take care of **our** own as well as all the others that did not take care of **their** water?"* Pouring it on the ground to have green lawns or spraying it in the air to grow **god/notes** will be stories we tell our grand kids,,, if we get a chance. Farmers in California reportedly use 80% of all the water and I'll bet 70% is lost to evaporation. They must find another way to grow **god/notes**.

But there are things we could do now to change how we treat this **Blue Gold**. The Hoover Dam would have to be closed and that water that we permit to flow into the sea will be kept to drink and grow food **not** to make electricity. We can live in the dark and drink or in a short time,,, live in the dark and **not drink**. Either way all the **blue gold** is going.

I suggest that we close the Hoover Dam now and save the water to drink and grow food responsibly. It could be turned into a museum and call, Gods Example of Abundant Antiquity Greed.

When the good Christians and others came to this land they all but wiped out the beaver, apparently to fill a new style need for hats. It is said that any place you find black fertile soil, you will find beavers one built dams to hold back clean water, thereby encouraging more life to grow. We are only now beginning to understand the full value of these small indigenous creatures and permitting them back into our lives as they save water for all of,,, we the living.

We must mimic the good beavers and dam up the small rivers and streams to save water and grow life. We must stop draining swamps and low lands and end the draining of fresh water into the sea. But as we slow water's pace or completely hold it back for some, the supply for others will end. We know this in Florida and have for years been reversing the damage done in the past, now saving the **Blue Gold**.

Reportedly we (America took over for the French) dug and built the Panama Canal to fill a need for war ships and then gave it away. We need another such project to help feed this nation and to help build a new style of farming from salt water that I understand will grow food. I am proposing large canals or tunnels to create a salt lake out of Salton Lake and Death Valley.

This influx of salt water will turn this dry hot land into a cooler wet climate and improve things for all creatures as it will help make rain from evaporation. We cut down all the trees for money and jobs and we now need to replace them.

Banzai Land

Background: I recall seeing a report back in the 70's that China was taking any and all trash for cash. Big corporations (mostly American) could bring their unwanted garbage that could not be dumped in their countries, or would cost too much to dispose of, to China for a fee. Any garbage at all was welcomed for a price. China got the trash and they got the cash. They also got pollution of ground water and cancer. More recently it was reported that China is the largest E-waste or electronic waste dumping ground in the world. This trash comes from developed countries (America) **illegally under UN conventions,,,** that don't want to pay to recycle it properly. This so called recycled material (many believe it is not actually being recycled) lines the streets in great piles, paves the roads and covers the river banks for miles in some areas (polluting their water and air). It was also reported that people that sit by fires all day and burn the solder from computer boards don't live long lives,,, allegedly it is five years before cancer fills their lungs.

The Fukushima nuclear power plant found on the east coast of Japan has for years now been dumping radioactive waste into the Pacific Ocean and that radioactive waste has been allegedly making its way around the coast line of Alaska and Canada and now down to the American coast.

This man-made calamity has brought much death and destruction to their country and we are now seeing deformities in small insect life and plants after only a few years. Their uncontrolled dumping of radioactive waste into the Pacific Ocean has now amassed a dump site at or near the size of the United States and is growing every day.

From the outside, Japan's crises management teams' solution to this radioactive waste appear to be, **just dump it into the ocean**. But they are trying to control it, only the leaks appear to be coming from everywhere.

Global Financial Super Heating

The airborne release of radioactive waste has resulted in mutations in food plants the likes of which have never been seen before. The Japanese government is in panic mode and trying to clean the land of the radioactive waste; but every time it rains the water and mud that come from the hills above pollutes the land below that they had just cleaned. And what to do with all the mounds of all that radioactive waste they have acquired?

At the same time Japan and China are in a heated dispute over some small islands in the East China Sea called the Senkaku Islands. There is no way to properly fix this that I can think of so I would like to offer a **comical solution** to these two problems. First off Japan could change the uninhabited islands from pointy mountain ranges sticking out of the sea to the shape of large bowls by taking off the tops and pushing the earth to the outer rims. Then removing all the radioactive waste from their homeland and piling it in the bowls. When they have filled up the bowls with this pollution just hand over the title and the keys to China with its new name,

Banzai Land.

Of course they cannot do this, but for me it is fun to think of. This type of corporate dumping of unwanted polluted land is not a new idea. It is sad to think, their pollution is going to be with us for a long time as it circles the globe spreading its mutations and birth defects and endless death.

Recently it has been reported that the outbreak of Starfish Wasting Disease may have been caused by Fukushima for, allegedly, its radiation is working its way down the coast of the United States or will soon be. Also the Hanford Site (home of the first nuclear weapons, Fat Man and Little Boy) found on the Columbia River in Washington State has been leaking radiation onto the ground and now it may be in the river dumping into the Pacific Ocean. However there have been outbreaks of this disease before, some dating back to the 1970s, the beginnings of records for this sort of thing.

This is the first drawback to the new water used to fill the Salton Sea and Death Valley, for it will come from this radioactive dump site source (Pacific Ocean). But by the time the filling of these two lakes starts, we could hope Japan will have this under control (unlike America and the Hanford site,,, it's only been 70 years) and the radioactive waste will be moving around the globe and will be replaced with cleaner water from the south. *This is a real pipe dream*.

However one looks at it, this Christian led government has not stopped or cleaned any part of the Hanford Site since the end of WWII that I know of. Yes they have spent money but not one drop has been cleaned to my knowledge. For the most part it has been left to the elements for over 70 years.

Global Financial Super Heating

Los Alamos National Laboratory (Project Y) in New Mexico doing classified work towards the nuclear weapons,,, another hot spot, is at an altitude of 7,500 feet, well above sea level. This would not affect the new salt sea, but what of all the testing out in the desert?

Jornada Del Muerto Desert is home of the **Trinity** (code name) of the testing of nuclear weapons by the United States. Also known as the **Manhattan Project** or **White Sands Proving Ground**,,, (proving what, I am not sure) or the **Alamogordo Bombing and Gunnery Range**, all sitting at or about 7,000 feet above sea level. So the new proposed Salton Sea should be safer from the war mongers' and money takers' pollution (radiation).

The Yucca Mountain Nuclear Waste Repository,,, what a nice name of a hole in the earth that is to hold trash from **The BIG 3**,,, paid for by the rest of us. This hole in the earth was to be in Nevada about 80 miles from the Las Vegas Valley and sits some 6,700 feet above sea level. It is part of the Nuclear Waste Policy Act amendments of 1987 (27 years ago) and reportedly has never been completed. So, as I understand, all the power plants in the United States store their trash <u>**ON SITE!**</u> Yes right next to your home and your drinking water. At any time these tubs of death will open up and each will be like the Fukushima disaster. For those of you that don't know,,, this is **very, very, very bad!**

The good part is America has laws to protect us (somewhat) from **The BIG 3** (for now) and you can see how well it is working. Now move your thinking to other countries that don't have our laws in place and things like Fukushima come to mind, where they are storing this nuclear waste in steel tubs that are bolted not welded together and you guessed it, are leaking into the ocean. I am willing to bet other countries just dump their radioactive waste on the ground and cover it with dirt. Or, worse yet, like America and Russia,,, just dump this nuclear waste into the sea. The toilet of the world.

Reportedly there are no less than 13 countries that are or have been dumping radioactive waste into the oceans. This has happened on the northwest coast of Russia where nuclear waste was dumped for years (and still may be); and on the west coast of America off California after WWII; and off the coast of England. I recall a report of this American Christian government dumping 5 nuclear submarines off the coast of California but can now find no such reports. **Look up 'Ocean disposal of radioactive waste'** *- it's quite an eye-full.*

We don't need to worry about governments starting a nuclear war with all their bombs,,, the war is over and those bombs have been dropped. The ghost of Little Boy and Fat Man have hit their targets all across the world,,, we are just waiting for them to explode. The rotting carcasses of their tubs of death will open up as the money runs out and there will be no place for any of us to hide,,, not even the 1%-ers.

For the most part life will go on with a new mix of birth defects across the board and only the creatures that live long lives (normally) will have their lives cut short,,, like man. Old age for us humanoids will most likely be 40 years and death will come from some type of cancer,,, brought to you by,,, **The BIG 3**.

Global Financial Super Heating

Chapter Eight

Surviving

Global Financial Super Heating

Global Financial Super Heating

If going forward we do nothing, how does each one of us survive in such a new and hostile world, which is coming and coming very soon? It helps if we look at it in sections, past, present and future. What has worked in the past will most likely work in the future.

Only this future is like nothing we have ever faced before. This future is coming at us very fast and will hit very hard when it comes,,, if we act now or do nothing. The damage to the earth by man is done and it is hard to determine truth from lies and all the fiction fed to us by the American Federal Dis-information Department.

Death, destruction, and abandonment will become the norm, as we simply turn a blind eye to others to save our own. Food and **Blue Gold** will become the future quests, as a good part of all business and the banking and sectors of government will collapse. But not any part of **The BIG 3** for they will get richer and live on as we move under their control under **Martial Law**,,, as we, the people, are to become,,, **guilty until proven innocent**. (Like the RIS now.)

All that we once knew will be gone as we all look back in time at the good old days when we could think freely and not have government tracking chips. Our children will listen to the old ones tell stories of a place now gone like the elders from Bikini Islands also known as the Bikini Atoll. America still pays to take care of these people to this very day and will for a long time into the future or until America is no more.

History; Bikini Atoll Islands is about 3.4 square miles and the America government moved the indigenous people off their pristine land. From 1946 to 1958 this tiny island became a nuclear testing platform setting off no less than 23 nuclear devices rendering the land uninhabitable - the radioactive fallout just dumping in to the sea.

Past

The **Roman Empire** started per historians, with an emperor called Augustus in the Christian year of 27 BC and ended in 467 AD. One cult religion sprang up from another, celebrating a most strange event, seems a human being became a god,,, again.

Apparently and as offensive as this may be for some, spiritual people started to listen to stories of this bastard *(also called whoreson, law of England and Wales, father did not marry the mother)* child of a virgin *(neat trick)* that was executed for crimes he committed and this cult rose to power in the fourth century. Two hundred years before that, the Romans fed these people to the lions for fun and sport, but some say, *cruelly*, they missed a few. Their lunacy religion grew and spread like all religious cancer, across the land and their new stolen religion with their new dead Jew man-god, became the Romans' newest god. Eventually and unfortunately it replaced all the other gods of that time *(my favorite being the Sun god)*.

So why bring this up? Because there are parallels that cross times that apply to today's dilemmas and may become part of our future. For I can find four that stand out clearly from this time, that can and do point us forward in time from this point,,, 2014.

1. People only pretend to pay taxes as spending was out of control.
2. Multiple wars with neighbor countries to steal their wealth.
3. Invading countries that had done nothing to them to power the war machine.
4. A single deadly religion (Christianity) taking over the government.

The **French Revolution** reportedly saw the beginnings of a democratic rule, preceded the start of the seven year war in 1756. The start of the American war with England started in 1775 to 1783 and was aided with funds from the French that could ill afford it. In 1778 the French declared war against Great Britain in support of the colonies. 1785 is the start of their financial crisis. In 1787 the archbishop (Christian) of Toulouse was appointed chief minister of the state. The financial collapse was soon to follow with the invention of the Guillotine.

1. Spending money was out of control.
2. Multiple Wars.
3. The invasion of other countries that did nothing to them to steal their wealth.
4. Religion (Christianity) spread into the government taking it over. Let the killing begin.

The next one that comes to mind is **Germany** after World War I. To help pay off their debts from this war with several countries (as I understand it) they just started printing money and **hyperinflation** or **super devaluation** rose and it would take a wheel barrow of paper money to buy a loaf of bread. Some would burn the money to cook and keep warm. Their currency had next to no value. One man rose to power with revenge on his mind and his desire to spread his good Christian beliefs. **(Jewish deicide)**

Global Financial Super Heating

Gott mit uns, (God with us) was on their belt buckles, as each man marched off to war spreading their good acts of their God.

"We tolerate no one in our ranks who attacks the ideas of Christianity. Our movement is Christian."

Reportedly a quote from Adolf Hitler, October 27, 1928 and once more there are parallels that jump out at you,,, if you look.

1. Mismanagement of the country's paper money.
2. Multiple wars.
3. Invaded countries that did nothing to them, to steal their wealth to fund Hitler's religious war enterprises.
4. A single religion (Christianity) took over the government of all the people.

The **United States of America**; founded in 1776 and partly paid for its war with borrowed money from France. *(Like in-laws I don't know if they ever paid it back.)* To help grow a new nation they would need more money and so they bought a printing press and started printing U.S. dollars backed by Spanish silver (stolen South American slave silver) and that ran out quickly. So to help things move quicker for this newly formed government, it just started printing more money backed with nothing. Today we call that fraud or a Federal Reserve note. If you or I did this they would haul us away and we would go to jail, for only **The BIG 3** can freely perpetrate such a crime.

Reportedly in 1788 the first religious chaplains were permitted into our government in spite of the first amendment to the Constitution, **Separation of Church and State**. The ignorance and cancer of this cult started in this year to decay the newly founded government regardless of their best attempts to keep all religious wacko's out.

This Christian cult cancer grew and popped up many times until more recently it was reported in 1954-55 under the code name Operation Passage to Freedom, whereby the United States transported only North Vietnam Christians to the safety of South Vietnam under the loving eyes of **the prime minister, a Roman Catholic**. Our tax dollars and American blood spilled to spread the word of this dead Jew man-god.

The Vietnam war was all about helping France re-colonize this land after WWII and for Americans,,, spreading Christianity. Over 58,000 Americans paid the price for this god with their lives, not to mention what we (American/Christians) did to the indigenous people.

Then in 1960 John F. Kennedy, the first Catholic president, was elected and there was dancing in the streets of Christian land. At this point religion and the war machine were well entrenched and he gave them legitimacy. However, allegedly, one of Kennedy's goals was to end the longest war (up to that time) that America had ever experienced and three years later **they** put a bullet in his head. *(See the Fourth Bullet Dealey Plaza,,, James Taque)*

After President Kennedy's murder or **The BIG 3** coup, the war lords must be served and we marched to war ever stronger and at every turn spreading Christianity as they kill those that stand in their way, Muslims, Buddhists and the dreaded atheist communists,,, **the Reds**.

*Would America have invaded, would they have killed and would they have tried to set up another new puppet government, if there were no Christian running this **American** government to begin with? Some believe the Vietnam War was a religious war against atheism. (Atheism does not require GOD to help or govern people. They don't need God to do the right things. But religious people do.)*

After September 11, 2001 (911) America has been on a one way road to ruin, using other people's money, to spread these so called Christian values, that so many believe **must be forced** on all **(because they can)**. For you see it does not matter whose money they use or who they kill as long as the end result is, they are spreading Christianity,,, at all and any costs.

The America Christian Supreme Court on May 9, 2014 frighteningly ruled that it is legal to start <u>government</u> meetings with prayers to God. The justices used such words as, "Jesus Christ" and "Christians" as part of their decision (are not ISIS or Al-Qaeda also religions?). Are they showing us all what God they support and are willing to force upon the rest of us? *"You will become Christian or we will cut off your arm."* **They do it because they can.**

This brings to my mind one query, and that is, what if this court were deciding if the religion that was speaking to citizens, via our government meetings was Al Qaeda or ISIS,,, would their vote have been the same? Justice Kennedy reportedly said *"prayers should be seen as ceremonial and keeping with the nation's traditions."* Then why do we have **Separation of Church and State** in the constitution,,, if not to have separation of church and state? Christianity has completely taken over this government. Are we then all doomed to their whims of lunacy?

This clearly flies in the face of the first amendment to the constitution and shows us all that there has been another Christian osmosis coup and our government is no longer for **all** people,,, just the chosen Christians. *(Very scary.)*

1. Mismanagement of the countries money.
2. Multiple wars
3. Invaded countries (Iraq) to steal its wealth (oil) reportedly to fund the war (never did). Then enter into two more wars. America is now all over the globe killing Muslims.
4. A single religion (Christianity) took over the government.

Present

There are several factors that must be taken into consideration as we look into the present. One is the population of the planet. Reportedly in the 1500s the population was 450 million people. It took three hundred years to double and became close to one billion people on the globe. Then in just about one hundred years it double once more to around two billion bringing us to the 1960s. Then in just around <u>fifty years</u> there was an unbelievable growth in people bringing us to present day with an estimated number of total people sharing this small space to <u>seven billion people</u>. All needing food to eat, clean water to drink and a warm place to live while having more and more babies and under the Christian master anti-abortion laws,,, many are unwanted.

Christians see abortion as the taking of a life and they are willing to kill as many people as needed to stop it. They are forcing **their** religion on the rest of us and the consequences are devastating. Before legalized abortion we had the **coat hanger abortions** that were less than safe. After legalized abortions in the 1970s an unexpected result happened within the United States. Crime rate started to drop because people were not having unwanted children. Only thing is it takes 20 years

133

to show the end results of ending abortion in a state, with an upward turn in crime. Forced Christian laws will create more crime with unwanted babies that are to be paid for with state dollars, via Christian laws. If Christians want these babies, let them pay for them, don't push the Christian bills off on the rest of us.

As the worst of our society rises to the top, becoming politicians, or poli-Christians, willing to say anything and do anything to be in power and keep their jobs, they are controlled by the ones with the money and influence. It looks like the warmongers (armament manufacturers) will feed and fan the flames of **all** religions to divide us, so the Christians can kill those that disagree with them. As we all stop looking at this world we live in as a place to enjoy, share, care for and help each other, but instead, a stepping stone from which to eventually leave (completely destroyed by man) and spend eternity with one god or another,,, take your pick,,, the arguments are comical at best, we all lose. The damage done to the earth by proponents of God and war (same thing), who only focus on the next life and leave the clean-up of the earth to one of their almighty Gods, is great. But what is to be left when these wackos kill themselves or each other off completely?

We all sit back, do nothing and watch as one god is forced on people over another. In the 1500s the invaders of South America told the indigenous people, *"accept our god or we will chop off your arms*." Reportedly in one day they did just that to 400 people. Their god took over and rules to this day controlling these people. Religion is all about control. And the war industry (war mongers) control God (Christians) walking hand in hand leaving death and destruction in their wake for money and power,,, and of course god.

But what of the stewardship of the planet and what we are leaving behind for those that survive,,, the **Meek**? Our resources are being stripped clean by the greedy, so the very few can line their nest with piles of green paper or **god/notes**. The land, air and oceans are gutted, leaving death, destruction, and poison behind for those who will survive (if any) to pay the price to try to clean it all up. All this is for war, greed, and some god.

As we all stand on the edge of man's climb up from the primeval mental muck and mud we all wallowed in, we are now poised at the edge of a great cliff overlooking the black abyss of our future. We are blinded to the brilliance of the darkness, this future will **incuse** for all time. What mark are we the **plastic people** to leave behind for those that dig up our remains 1,000 or 10,000 or 100,000 years from now?

Future

As I said before, one mostly only need look to the past to see the future. Every man, woman, and child on this planet will see the effects of focusing on a god, the afterlife, and trust in paper to have value with all the corrupt governments and those lying politicians lining their pockets.

For those in the know, it is a very simple system that has been used and followed before. It's an old game with new players. They have stripped the land of all its resources, polluted the ground, air and water that we all share and now have stripped the economy and are abandoning the once great ship called United States of America for greener lands. By greener I mean, those people that don't know, they are green (uneducated to the **BIG 3**) as to what is to come.

The war mongers will move on to those greener pastures consuming as much **god/notes** as they can carry, but carry where?. The wars will continue as they each will spread their god's word and kill those that will not bend to their gods will, for there is only one god and the others that have the wrong god must be killed. You can see what a great business plan this is, for if one side starts to kill the other side, they must kill back. To some 911 was revenge for what Christians have done in the past. It was not an attack,,, it was a defensive act.

Day one
It could start one of three ways.

Way one

This Christian American government may present us with their best stuffed shirt and they will announce, *"The federal government will make a tiny adjustment in the dollar's value and to help us reduce the national debt we are cutting the god/note green back by only 15%".* **This is one way they will F*** those that bought our government's bonds or invested in American money.** If you had $1,000.00 in the bank, you now have $850.00 of buying power,,, over night. The price of food will go up by more than 15% because the suppliers cost have also gone up by 15% and therefore you can expect to see food prices jump by much more. More likely a jump in price of 50% to 100%, cutting the value of your **god/notes** in half, as the price of everything grows and I'll bet gasoline will more than double in price.

This jump or doubling overnight is a knee jerk reaction by big business to the true cost of the devaluing dollar by the government. They are reacting to the fear that the dollar's drop in value will continue and they must charge more now to offset any additional drops in its value that are to come. This panic and hording will spread into all sectors, *"if I can sell it for one dollar today, I can hold it and sell it for two dollars tomorrow. I will just wait."*

Way two

Every country, government, investor and 401K will pull away from buying government bonds. The rate paid to investors of bonds will go up to entice them as more money is paid out in interest. This will force the federal government to slow spending money it does not have and it will collapse or just start printing more paper money to pay its bills (the trillion dollar coin) as it tries to calm us all down, *"don't worry we have it all under control. Remember **(gott mit uns)** God is with us."*

Every country that is holding our bonds will see them drop in value over night as they are asked to take a haircut, (cutting the value of the bonds paid back to the investor) by 25%, 50%, 75% or 100%. Their income and worth (from bonds) in each bond-holding country will plummet and they will be driven into a depression of some type, caused by Christian America. **This is the second way this government will F*** those that bought these bonds or trusted in the U.S. dollar (god/notes).**

The stock markets across the globe will most likely crash because everyone trusted this colonizing Christian government's **god/notes**. If you have money there (shark markets, bonds, 401k's, **god/notes**) you could become broke and living on the streets. Or worse yet,,, does **The BIG 3** have other plans for those that can't accept the new order of things or complain or people that write books talking of the way things may become under the new order.

Way three

China could grow tired of paying for this Christian American meddling in their back yard (they buy our bonds so we can send war ships to encircle them) and pull the rug out from under us all by causing a financial tsunami and call in our debts. They will be losing money doing this but it will get the Christian Americans and their distortive war mongering ways out of their back yard and they can enlarge their influence in this,,, their region.   **This is the third way this government will F*** those that bought these bonds and hold these god/notes as something of value.   Christian colonizing or sometimes called American interest has its price.**

This will be the strongest and hardest crash for everyone, as American enemies enjoy seeing this Christian government crash. As of today the Saudis have join China and other countries in setting a new currency for oil (no longer the U.S.A. dollar) and their new prices for oil will help bring America crashing further to its knees. The Saudis are now dumping the U.S. dollar and, as I understand, have bought or invested in the European banking system (moving away from the USA). They know it is coming or they will help it to come. Russia will gleefully join in, as will other enemies of this America the Christians have made, and the unraveling will begin starting with Israel as Palestine gets long-overdue help regaining its stolen land. Please note,,, **The BIG 3** are still on top, doing just fine.

These examples of currency do not take in to account the natural path of global warming and Mother Nature's revenge. Entire countries will face this devastation and those fragile governments and their god/notes will collapse. Those starving masses will be angry and on the move coming to a country near you.

The first weeks

Regardless of how it happens, (in these three examples) the costs of goods plus food will go up across the globe because of the downward fall or adjustment in the **god/notes** and corporations will be forced to make cutbacks. The money once spent on luxury items will be used for necessities as each person cuts back their spending. Manufacturers will not need supplies because they are not selling so they stop building products and as this all grinds to a halt people will be laid off.

I can see there will be bank runs all over the globe for people will want to keep their hands on what money they have instead of trusting it to those with a reputation of theft and mismanagement, the banksters. It may not have much value but better under the bed than with all these corporations as they crash. And who will bail them out this time? If this Christian America is broke, (as it is) if no one will loan America money, (the government) the military will just take over. Some type of Christian **Marshal Law** (that seems to be in place) could be enforced on us just like it is today on the people in Thailand and Egypt. And it will be years,,, if ever, before the military will reinstall a new puppet leader they can control, like Johnson or Ragan or Bush or Obama.

Is this the direction Christian America is moving? The president, (Obama and others before him) seems to be passing all manner of laws via **Executive Orders** that empower one person, one master, one ruler, one king, in spite of the Constitution of this country. As though it were being modified for a smooth takeover by one Deity, maybe **The BIG 3** will now **not** have to answer to anyone anymore. Is that their plan? What am I saying,,, they don't really answer to anyone now. Every aspect of it (Constitution) is being rewritten before our eyes,,, and we do and say nothing,,, but go along with the flow. As George W. Bush said, *"you're with us or you're against us."* And the men in the military are,,, just follow orders.

Restaurants, beauty salons, barber shops, repair shops, construction, builders, glass repair shops, car lots, ice cream stores, and other small businesses, the backbone of this country, will feel it first in a drop off or complete end of all sales. *"Don't need employees if we are not selling. I will call you if we get busy".* Oh yes,,, and if things are getting bad,,, we had better postpone that vacation and/or business trip and keep that money for the future or for food as more hording occurs. Fear, justified or not, will only make things much worse.

The first months

We could see everything grind to a halt, as the layoffs will hit across the board, across the country, and across the globe. States will be inundated with the recently unemployed and will not be able to afford to care for the masses. This and bad management in the past by our state leaders will cause each state to file bankruptcy, for they just don't have the money as sales tax dollars disappear.

But these leaders do have nice homes and nice offices in nice new government buildings and big Golden Umbrellas. If there is no money for unemployment, there will be no money for the state welfare system, no state health care and no free rides including retirement packages. When it

Global Financial Super Heating

happened to California, back in the 70s (as I recall) they paid their employees with IOUs, *"how do I pay my bills and eat with this?"* one asked.

Plant closings and business bankruptcies will help to inundate the federal courts, but for some that can't afford the attorney fees, they will just walk away leaving it for the banks and states to clean up. The courts system will become overwhelmed and it too will have cutbacks in its budgets. Court time could end up taking years or decades for settlements, if at all. Or the military could just take over and seizure of all property would occur and we would become more like our enemies to this newly empower **Marshal Law** government, those dreaded communist,,, the REDS. I like to think of us as becoming the new Citizen Terrorist (people that openly complain while working in the government work camps).

If you can barely take care of your bills now, think of what life will be like if and when money drops in value, just a small amount. You will, and must, make more cuts. One of the first cuts I see would be student loans, which now top over 1.2 trillion dollars of debt primarily owed to the federal government, all by individuals. The colleges got paid so they don't care.

The next will be your house payment, rent, and cable television. Power and phone bills will be paid if you can until that money runs out. Then those two will join the non paid bills for you must have food and water.

Global Financial Super Heating

More gas stations will close as the fuel costs rise. I can see 50% to 75% of these **foreign owned** stations will become boarded up as they, the foreign owners, return home to join their families with stories of how funny the ignorant Christian Americans are and how bad things have become for all those Christians. They will be passing out candy in the streets, once more celebrating, as to how the American Christian beast is brought to its knees.

Life will become much better for them as they return to a more prosperous, non military, non colonial country, unlike America, that has been in a downward spiral and still is, trying to police the world. They may have to return home via ships.

Plane travel and road trips will for the most part end as money loses value and disappears from the street ending up back in the government's hands as it did in 1929. Coins and small denomination currency will become novelties as they did in Germany at the end of WW1,,, (much like they are now in this country). The highways will be free of cars, and primarily for the rich, and the airports will clog with jets that have no travels and no money to buy jet fuel to move them. They will join the bankrupted and be pushed to the sides of the runways, as only the few rich people will be able to afford to travel by air, in much smaller planes of the future.

And now we can turn our eyes to the heavens above and see the stars like never before as cities turn off street lights because they can't pay the bills. Murders, rapes, and theft will go off the charts as cities can't pay their employees. Blocks will burn for there are no fire fighters and no money for fuel to get there. Trash will line the streets like we see in third world countries and disease will come in waves of outbreaks. Big cities will be the worst place to be in this collapsing future, but as for small towns, people know each other and are more apt to help.

Your county sheriff will announce he can no longer protect you in your home and tell you to carry a gun at all times to defend yourself, *"shoot to kill and there will be no investigation."*

Then the heat will be turned up. With no global shading, (**jet con trails polluting the upper atmosphere**) the sun's ultraviolet rays will have nothing to bounce off of and now come straight down to the surface of the earth. There will be less pollution from cars so city streets will hold the heat of the day and water will evaporate much faster. Global warming will go into high gear and become

Global Financial Super Heating.

Temperatures across the globe could rise on average by five to ten degrees if we do nothing but follow these god people,,, guided by the real power players. The food we produce will burn up in the fields as the desert starts to cross the lower United States and the rivers and lakes continue to dry up.

One year and more

If nothing is done to stop this and I do not mean burning less fossil fuels, for (I believe) it is way too late for that. I am speaking of replacing the pollution from the jets in the upper atmosphere to deflect the suns heating rays, the planet will only get hotter. The glaciers that help cool the planet will melt faster and faster as entire regions of the world that rely on them will have no water, for it has drained into the sea and they be relying on rain water only. Wars over water will occur and the military will need to guard the home front from the invasion of the thirsty (that did not take care of their water) all over the globe.

I can see one country diverting its river to a reservoir and cutting off another country's water. Such a situation could happen in Tibet where China rules and could cut off India of its water.

Several questions I have would be, when all the water melts from the north and south poles, it all will go into the oceans but because the world spins faster at the center than at the top, will the centrifugal force spin the water to higher points on the equator than on the poles? The weight of the water shifts from the top and bottom to the sides and would go from a solid to liquid. Would

Global Financial Super Heating

centrifugal force spin the water with the moon pulling at it into a wall of water circling the globe at 5' or 10' or more as a (moon lifted) high tide? We all know there will be more water; this is over the top of the new predicted levels that I question. And if the top of the world is lighter and the center thicker will the world spin slower? **Will we see 25 hour days?**

The rich or one percent-ers will move from the desert regions of America and head north to the new tropical regions of Canada. I believe because Florida is surrounded on three sides by water, it will have rain to help replace the aquifers and the influx of people looking for water will grow at an alarming rate. There will be an invasion of the thirsty. Will the state guard the borders and turn the thirsty away with their buckets in hand?

The airplane manufacturers that build fighter jets to supply the defending foreign economies (from the newly displaced) with war machines, maybe one of the only businesses to do well in the future. Their wealth will buy up every supplier as labor costs struggle to keep up with the ever falling dollar. Yes, you may make $1,000.00 a week but that will not buy food to feed your family, let alone pay your other bills.

Water filtration and water desalination plants will do fine for those that can afford it. As cities cannot pay to clean water it will become up to each person. Have you ever seen the water that comes from the tap in Miami? It was brown in the

80s, but maybe they have cleaned it up by now. *It was not something you wanted to drink.*

I just think the population will not grow at the pace predicted because the food will be disappearing. Less than 10% of the once grand and endless fish supplies of the oceans remains. Some think in less than ten year we will see this dry up and as in Africa; people will turn inward for food killing everything that moves. Cats, dogs and birds will become things of the past, as only man walks the land in search of food,,, even if its radioactive.

This hunger will only grow and the weak and old will die off first. But what a waste of good meat you say. It was reported in the mid 1800s the newest members of the Mormons were heading to the promise land, to be closer to their **new god** and the holy one (a man) that could guide them, when they were stranded in a winter storm and stuck for that winter in the mountains. There in the freezing cold, they were starving and when the sick died the families did not go hungry. These good holy God fearing people on their way to join other godly people,,, did **eat** their loved ones. **Cannibalism** is a thing that has been with us for as long as we can track history and is with us now today. Even though we pretend it is not and we look the other way.

Within some holy books it is written and has been rewritten many times, *"unless you eat the flesh of the son of man and drink his blood, you have no life. Whoever eats my flesh and drinks my blood will have eternal life."* As a vegetarian I can say I will not be joining these people in **their** afterlife,,, this religion is just sick, sick, sick.

So I can see cook books on how to cook people hitting the market. *How to best Serve Man* is one title I would use. Oh now don't be shocked, cannibalism has been with us from the beginnings of time, 6,000 years ago. No wait that's the god peoples' calendar, it been with us longer than that.

As the Christian government ruling America collapses and retreats from world Christian colonialism, colonizing for Christ would become the responsibly of other Christian led countries. It will be up to someone else to kill the Muslims and Jews for American Christians have done their best and now need time to recover from this depraved adventure into god land.

They did their part by giving American borrowed tax money to the Pakistan government that in turn gave much of it to Al Qaeda so they could buy arms from the war profiteers and kill the Christian Americans and their own people that are not godly enough. The war mongers will simply turn to others, like ISIS, that will kill for their god and have the money to pay for it. This new terrorist cult is now killing anyone that is not Muslim enough with Christian supplied war machinery. They then enslave the females and sell them for top dollar. Jesus must be very happy with his good loving followers,,, for Muslim is killing Muslim.

Global Financial Super Heating

Would this be what gets Americans to turn off the T.V. put down their can of beer and that bag of potato chips and get them off of their couches and onto their feet rising up to rebel against this Christian corrupt government? Will we see a revolution like the one the French had as their leaders squandered away all the money in the 1700s? Will we hunt down the rich killing them and their children just for fun and sport and a good meal? Will the imbalance that is coming be that grand? When there is no food and there is no water, they, the masses, will come after someone. Is this what the American government or **The BIG 3** is preparing for?

I sometimes wonder, would the flesh of a super rich 1%-er, taste better than a poor person? I think yes, because they will have been fattened up for the slaughter with only the best of foods. I am going to work on my cook book that should include how to best butcher the rich and super rich. Then I want to work on a special healthy dipping sauce and I will call it *Green Poooo-pon, for the Rich and 1%ers*.

Of course I am joking because I am a vegetarian for the most part,,, but I could see myself giving up that life style for one meal of the rich and plentiful.

Chapter Nine

Preparing for the **Wild West Pandemics!!!**

Global Financial Super Heating

Where to begin? Well we could all put our heads down and pray to one of the gods to take care of all of this and that would be so easy, to put all of this manmade disaster that is to come, in the hands of the old man in the sky. Or we could cut off the arms of the non believers (voices that disagree with us) and burn the witches at the stake or impale them. That sounds like fun and has worked so well in the past,,, right? No wait,,, that has not worked in the past and is a dumb idea. But alarmingly I do not feel we are that far away from such things as I am still trying to look forward.

The best place to start for me is where I am right now May 2014, in a place called America and something we can do to help ourselves. I have always been a believer that the worst place you can keep your money is in money. Why would you ever put hard earned cash in the bank where it is drawing 00.25% interest when your money is dropping at today's rate of just under 3% per year (per the government)? Are you nuts?

What about the stock market,,, it is doing so well right now? I predicted the last crash only I was sure it would drop more than it did. I felt sure it would hit 3000 (it's true worth?), but did the government buy up the falling stock to stop it from hitting bottom (protecting the rich)? Reportedly today the stock market, or what I call the **shark market**, is rigged and a very dumb place to put your money. Unless you are one of the riggers or one percent-ers or one of the banksters that are exempt from the laws the rest of us must obey.

"So I can't keep my money in money, I can't keep my money in the bank and I can't keep my money in the rigged shark market,,, where then?"

Tangibles!

That which is real,,, something you can put your hands on,,, not a piece of paper from a government or shark market. Oil painting, works of art, old coins, antiques, collector cars, property, and best of all GOLD and SILVER. The world's true currency, that which at one time this and other government's paper money was backed. Before the clever idea of funny money or **god/notes, tangible** money was made with real silver and real gold. From a very stable time, with little or no devaluation of paper money backed with gold and silver to a time when money became **god/notes** and the system was changed forever, spiraling downward to its real value,,, nothing.

Now you should not run out in a panic and spend all your cash, for all I am saying is **think about tangibles** as an investment. If you own a piece of property and there is a big crash, everyone that owns a piece of property is in the same boat. It all has dropped in value the same amount as your neighbors, but it has some value. It does not become worthless unless it is in and part of the new desert that is to come. You can live on it, grow food on it and survive, and if it is paid for they can't (for the most part) come and get it and take it from you. Unless the president signs another Executive Order and empowers his office to take it all, for himself or his Deity and **The BIG 3**.

Warning; this is not financial advice as to where <u>you</u> should place your god/notes but an example as to how <u>I</u> invest. It is up to you, the reader, to choose your own path.

As some think industries will collapse like dominos, there will be few jobs for sure. Today all businesses are trying to think of ways to eliminate people and becoming very good at it. Pay on line, buy on line and computer phone calls are just a few ways to eliminate people and increase the bottom line. **I only buy from people and I try to only pay by check using the mail because it employs people.** If the dollar falls as hard as some think, there will be no money. The government will have it all as it did in the depression of the 30s. Bartering will become the new old currency.

So if there is no one in America that has money (but the super rich), who will buy my tangibles? Foreigners! They will be on us like flies on a carcass, stripping it clean of any value. As when England's paper dollar collapsed, the rest of us stepped in and bought as much as we could carry back to the states with us. They got our paper, and we got their tangibles. Paper (not real) going down in worth every day, tangibles (real) holding its own or going up in worth as others will want that one art, car, or property on the water, that there is and that you have. Things will always have value as long as there are people to buy them.

In the depression of 2007 you could see a good example of the wealth of America shipping overseas,,, if you only looked. Everyone seemed to have a boat in their yard with a loan on it. Can't pay your bills,,, let the boat go back to the bank; and that they did, and American boats and other toys went overseas in shipping containers at record speeds. Overnight a massive amount of American wealth went overseas,,, gone for good. But the banks got paper **god/notes,,,** from foreigners.

Global Financial Super Heating

This continues even today as our used cars are shipping overseas. The car auctions are full of foreigners buying up American wealth and taking it with them to other countries, driving up the price the rest of us pay. If our used products (real) are driving up prices, is that not a sign the rest of the world is showing us, how much the American paper dollar or **god/notes** are really dropping in value?

If you doubt this, look at the news reports from overseas and you see all the foreigners driving big American cars. Where do you think they got them? The half price sale in America brought to you by big business and this government and **The BIG 3**.

Are the car manufactures smarter than we think? Do they and other super corporations, see the writing on the wall that we don't? Is that why they have moved their manufacturing plants overseas? At first I believe it was to break the strangle-hold the unions had on the car manufacturers. It is widely believed that the car industry in the 70s did this to break the back of the greedy unions,,, and it did. But now look at where they (car industries) mostly all are, overseas with their wealth away from this distortive Christian led government. Their dollars are safe from a crumbling corrupt government with one agenda,,, war for God. Did corporate America see this over 40 years ago, how Christian war mongers were moving in,so they moved out?

Global Financial Super Heating

Did big business (like oil) cause the collapse that is to come or did they just go along with the other big corporations (oil) that were using this Christian led government to invade countries that did nothing to us,,, but have oil and/or be Muslim? It looks to me, an outsider,,, Christians got to spread Christianity by killing Muslims and the oil companies got oil and the war industries got to sell bombs. **The BIG 3.** It would not be the first time a country invaded and killed for money and god. England, France, Germany, Spain, Russia, Japan, China, Mongolia and yes America,,, just to name a few.

All marching off to war with God on their side as they killed, maimed, butchered, raped, and destroyed the inferior people,,, **because they can**. Implanting their god, their beliefs, their laws and their goods, (sometimes called **American interest**) thereby enriching their warmongers, the ones at the very top that are responsible for all the carnage that is to come.

I can hear the warmongers saying to the good Christians, *"We give you the people now you give them your god."* Hand in hand they walk together leading us all down this path to complete global destruction. God or all religions being led by power (oil) using warmonger industries to fulfill their greed. Oil uses God that uses warmongers.

$ $ $ $ $ $ $ $ $ $ $ $ $ $ $ $ $ $ $ $

The Big Three

The **first** and at the top of all power plays and power grabs and behind most all events is **OIL** or POWER like electricity and **MONEY** like banksters. This elusive giant has a face and some believe it can be found within secretive organizations like the Free Masons. Allegedly under the pretenses of doing good they take over all business by farming work to each other,,, exclusively. They have moved into government long ago and as I understand Jimmy Carter, not a member at the time, had to become a member before he could become president of the United States. They have that much power! Other secret organizations are out there and one name that comes to mind is the Skull and Cross Bones,,, (I did not make that up). These power men are well hidden and well protected and will require much work if you are to try to look them up.

The **second** of the **BIG 3** is the armaments manufacturers and the **warmongers** (army, navy, marines and air force. If you build it they must use it,,, for what is the point to having a new killing machine and then not put it to use,,, killing? Reportedly five high ranking generals in the United States military fought with President,,, John F. Kennedy over ending the Vietnam War and at that time he fired them. Their retaliation (the military) was to put a bullet in his head. His replacement Lyndon Johnson, rehired the generals and micro managed the war's escalation. Over 58,000 American soldiers died and countless indigenous people of this region, to use war armaments and make money for the warmongers as this destabilized region was primed and ready for Christianity to be spread. All under the watchful eye of the secret societies,,, enriching themselves.

The **third** in this well orchestrated or well oiled machine is **RELIGION** and the mindless followers. The religious far right has been in the process of de-educating the masses within this country for some time now and with the blessings of the secret society. For you cannot control intelligent people, therefore you must keep them stupid and fearful. What better tools than God and death? *Afraid to live,,, afraid to die.*

Got mit uns
In God we trust
$ $ $ $ $ $ $ $ $ $ $ $ $ $ $ $ $

Are we about to pay the price for aggression and greed or for religion? Or is this the price we pay when we as a people look the other way permitting apathy to rule our lives. As we sit back in our ignorance and permit this Christian government to pick and choose whichever person and whichever law it wishes to prosecute and we say nothing. Some examples that come to mind are all the Banksters and all the Christian pedophiles the pope is protecting. **The question should be, is the fault in the god people or with non-religious or both? For to me the blood is on all our hands.**

If one looks closely, you can almost see the red horned beast standing behind each of the most recent popes grinning with his approval. The smell of sulfur is gagging and decent thinking people must turn away.

It's all about control, as it always has been over the centuries. Take over a government, force God on the people to control them, get their money, de-educate the masses (can't control smart people) and spread God to other countries to get their money. That is why Christians hate atheists (as well as other religions) so much, they can't control them. That is why Christians hate communism so much; it, allegedly, fairly cares for each person (without God),,, or so goes the theory. **That is why we have Separation of Church and State in America,,, or had.** Now we are all about to see why this <u>was</u> so important.

If you are a skeptic as to religion taking control over this government and picking laws and people it wishes to prosecute just look at recent news,,, just this year 2014,,, five months.

The law: It is a federal offense (and against the law in every state) to molest a child and it is against the law to protect that person by moving them from one state to another (aiding and abetting and interstate flight to avoid criminal prosecution).

The people: It was reported on January 17th this year 2014 that the pope defrocked 400 priests for sex abuse. **400!!!** During the first years of this last depression 08 and 09 I believe the Vatican removed over 170 priests for sex abuse. Are we now talking about over 570 child sex abusing men that they,,, and the pope are protecting. How many more are there that they are not telling us about,,, the ones that did not get caught or they are still protecting?

This **man** (the accused protector of pedophiles) calling himself the pope apparently refused to release their names (pedophiles) so they can be prosecuted in their respective countries. The pope is protecting pedophiles. **Who is worse**, the one that raped a helpless child scarring them for life or the one that protect the rapists under Gods name? **The Vatican/pope was ordered by the United Nations committee to release all their names (the pedophiles) at this time 2014.**

Reportedly john paul (an **alias** name for the pope) was faced with a pandemic outbreak of news of pedophiles in the church and he did his best to conceal and control the sex abuse scandal. All good qualities in a religious leader that we like to see,,, right? No wait,,, that makes him a criminal, a liar and a conspirator to cover up and conceal evidence of a crime against a child. And 2.5 billion people follow him and seek out his guidance.

Frightening,,, if it weren't so sad.

April 27th of this year 2014, it was reported that the current pope frances (an **alias** name) proclaimed the two proceeding popes, john the 23rd and john paul 2nd (also **alias** names if I have them

right) were to become **saints**.

I am not making this up!

Only problem is they are a little <u>light</u> on miracles. So I would like to offer my help in this department. I can think of one miracle they have overlooked and for me as a kind non-religious person, I offer it to all the Christians to consider. Both these popes should become saints (by Christian standards) because they cover up sex crimes against children and did not go to jail.

That is a miracle.

If it were you or me we would be wearing stripes, in leg irons and in solitary confinement for our participation for this crime. But not these two and all the others within their criminal organization, that eluded prosecution for their part and their criminal acts against us all. But mostly defenseless children suffer with a life sentence,,, at our silence hand. These Christians are resourceful people using the pretense of God, to protect them. We all say nothing and hide from these organized criminal kingpins as we would from some kind of a drug cartel or mafia. Their revenge would be swift and powerful. So let's not say a word and hope they don't rape us or kill us or use **their** justice system to get **us** with trumped up charges of crimes or law suits.

Let us all continue to fear life and fear death, with the worst of mankind, Christians and other holy people guiding us through life, as we all say nothing, perpetuating their crimes. These people are the worst of the worst and we say nothing.

Pandemics

We seem to be faced with pandemics of many types and must prepare for each one that may come our way. Each will require different action on our part to protect ourselves and our children as well as the future of man. If some of the points I make about the future are wrong the worst that would happen is you would be prepared.

The population will not grow much more because of some strains of influenza or other type of death brought to us by some little bug that will cross the globe in a matter of days. When a bad one hits it will be in every country that has a plane and an air port,,, if they are still flying. Let's look at the Middle East respiratory syndrome coronavirus or MERS-CoV, a pandemic that came from the Middle East and in a few days was in this county and could have been the Big One.

Ebola is another example of pandemics that can't be controlled. The **goody two shoes** of the world see the need to travel to Ebola land and offer some type of help. That is fine but don't come back. If you are infected with Ebola go live in another country but don't bring it (the disease) back here to kill a nation of people just because you want to serve some god. It's not right (exposing the rest of us to death) and it is not Christian (self-importance) feeling only you can make a difference.

Because this country is now run by the Christians they are going to expose us all to this disease **because they can**. The Ebola incubation period can be up to three weeks giving the good Christians plenty of time to bring the world this deadly disease.

Are these people nuts or are we,,, because we say nothing? The first dumbass we will call Dr. B. a good Christian and a member of some global Christian organization, contracted Ebola and fearing for **his** life exposed all of us to this deadly disease sometime in August of this year 2014. What did he think was going to happen? But to bring it back to

America,,, does he not know he could kill Christians as well. Or his own self importance (Christian) outweighs your life and mine.

Then in September of this year they shipped the second Christian to America with Ebola we will call her Miss W.,,, but why? She wanted to help and now she should pay the price,,, her life. But don't expose us all to this incurable disease just because you are a Christian.

In this same month a third nut job is brought back to America I will call him Dr. S. Each time the security seems to be less and less. Will the next one just get on an airplane and fly with regular people? As I am writing this book, that just came true in Texas, New York and a cruise ships this October of 2014 and now **states** are closing their borders,,, finally.

*These states are protecting the rest of us from the good Christians,,, something the federal government could not do,,, or did not want to do. Why would the federal government want a deadly disease to freely enter this country? How would this benefit **The BIG 3**? Who would gain and what would they gain by using the Christians in this way?*

I discovered that the hospitals that are taking these sick Ebola people are Christian hospitals. The next thing I discovered is each one has spent millions of dollars on laboratories design (so they think) to contain outbreaks. Like bombs that kill, they must be used.

Now let's try to bottom line this; religion (Christians) use its power over the government (Poli-Christians) to help make money for the powerful (1%-ers). If you build it,,, like bombs you need a war to use it. Ebola was prefect to be used as a test case for the 1%-ers to make money. That is why we were all exposed to this killer,,, it's for **god/notes,** so all may make more money. **They do this because they can.** But is there more behind what I can see and I can find?

Financial Pandemic

I would not take on new debt at this time unless it would be to invest in tangibles. I invest and sell all the time so I use OPM (other people's money) to make money. Some experts tell us the dollar is going to drop in value by a percent ranging from 10% to 25% depending on who you listen to.

But when you look at history, it shows us that paper money backed with nothing, as in **god/notes,** in the past has dropped in value much more than that. Closer to 50% to 75% may be a better figure in the short term, so it will not be all at once, but over a short time. I feel it may be closer to five to ten years away. It is going to happen, just hard to pick a day in the future. As in the past as I understand, Germany and the Soviet Union had to change their currency to stop the free fall as their dollar fell to zero value.

So I have chosen to keep my money in tangibles. As an example if you borrow $10,000.00 from the bank and buy the same amount of real gold, then the crash happens and gold hits the new highs (because it is real) they are talking about, you could be sitting on fifty to sixty thousand dollars or more. Just sell one brick and pay back the bank (with deflated dollars) and the rest is yours.

I am not recommending you do such a thing, but I use this as an example <u>only</u> to show you how gold is stable and paper money (god/notes) is not.

Now that is a lot of ifs, but people have been hedging their bets with gold for a lot of years. Just think!!! What is a better place to keep your earnings,,, paper or gold??? Gold will always be worth something for sure (it is stable); paper, on the other hand, you may just end up burning it to cook your food or heat your home - if you have either.

Medical, Plague Pandemic

The list of potential pestilences is long and scary and fills the mind with visions of death and destruction. Tiny things we cannot see, we cannot taste and we cannot smell could cross the globe in days taking with it hundreds of thousands of lives,,, if not more.

As I said before, this was just in the news this April,,, MERS-CoV found only in middle east (so they tell us) is now in the United States and infected others. It has a very high kill rate and comes from handling lamas. So be warned, don't eat any lama meat.

Ebola may indeed be the one that I have been talking about, for as of the middle of September this year 2014 the experts predict the outbreak will reach and kill half a million people before they can get it under control. It was just on the news this week of 9/15/14 that a doctor, (one of the goody-two-shoes god people) went over to Ebola land for a visit and exposed herself to this deadly disease (I am not sure why,,, perhaps for some self important or self gratification,,, Gods work) then she returned to this country. She,,, this very stupid doctor, just got on a plane and flew back to America possibly carrying this killer disease, with no regard for the rest of us. Perhaps that is the true meaning of Christianity = self serving. "I can do whatever I want because I am doing God's work."

The power of prayer

Regardless of the reason, I was stunned that she,,, a doctor, would do this and in my thinking of her ignorance, I may have missed the real reason. Perhaps she wanted to get firsthand experience in treating this disease in a third world environment. That way she can be prepared for what is to come to America and just how it will look. I think of her as Typhoid Mary and I will just call her Dr. TM.

Her comments at the end of this short report (aired on the news shows) really stunned me,,, she said, *"I was really surprised that no one stopped me from coming in (back to America) at the airport."* Now in her own words, we all can see that she **knew** what she was doing was **wrong** and yet she did it anyway. Dr. TM. <u>went right back to work,,, in a hospital,,, exposing all to Ebola</u>. Maybe in her self-importance she did not see a need to protect the rest of us because she is somehow protected with God's magical glow.

The insanity of government or **lack** of government with regards to Ebola is clear - if you are Christian you can bring down a nation killing millions of people if you are doing God's work. **They do it because they can.** Who has this power over government to make leaders look the other way and why? You must keep wondering who would benefit from such overwhelming death? The power behind all government actions is the beneficiary.

Super bugs

Superbugs that now live, breed, and grow, are found to thrive in hospitals where we go when we are sick. There is no cure, no medication and the weakest among us seems to be those that visit doctors the most and take all the prescriptions and antibiotics from the **Drug Dealing Doctors**.

Another good source of abundant antibiotics, reportedly, is from the food industry where they allegedly inject poultry and livestock and penned fish with large amounts of drugs that we in turn eat.

Our immune systems are depleted and we have no defense to kill these new super bugs. Reportedly Cuba has had free health care for years and their solution to most ailments is antibiotics. A super bug could wipe out a whole country in days.

The solution seems to be, don't live in a big city with international airports, don't take antibiotics and don't go to the hospital and don't listen to your doctor. <u>Of course this can't all be done and I am in no way recommending you become an agoraphobe.</u> I am saying you must watch what you eat, drink and the pills you ingest.

Killing for food

Killing for food is already happening across the globe and is not that far away from us and the financial crash that is coming brought to you by the American falling dollar. The start of the falling dollar will bring widespread shortages of food. It's going to get ugly. I can't count the number of people who have told me something like this, *"if you have a sandwich and my kid is hungry, I am getting that sandwich and my kid will eat."* These words are from good law abiding people.

All it will take is some type of super bug that kills a crop like rice and millions will starve.

Global Financial Super Heating

For example: We only grow one type of potato in this country on a large scale for the fast food market. One super bug or a fungus called Oomycete or more commonly known as the potato blight, that causes that food (potatoes) to rot in the ground, comes to mind. Such a famine hit in the mid 1800s in Ireland and if it should hit again, we all must turn to another type of food and that will cause a shortage across the globe.

The land in Ireland did, at that time (1844), grow sufficient amounts of food to feed all the people in the country preventing the mass starvation that took place. One million people died and a million more left their homeland, causing a reduction in the population of that country of up to 25%. But the suppressing invaders (England under Christian rule) took the food grown on Irish soil, grown by Irish people and shipped it home to their land (England), sold it for the almighty dollar and said to the Irish people during that starvation cyclic of 7 years, *"Let them eat grass"* and they did. Heartless words from good Christians,,, that still are burned deeply in memories of these people to this very day.

It happened then and it will happen now. *"Our country has no food and yours does, so we will take yours,,, **we do it because we can**,,, and you can eat grass."* So it is part of the Christian past, so it will become part of the future.

Many people I know are storing food, like rice, in their homes along with ammo to defend it.

Global Financial Super Heating

The government cannot take away your guns (at this time and under this current government) as they did in England, whose people are now defenseless from invaders, but they can stop selling bullets. It will become the wild west, only worse,,, people will be killing for food. Now I don't just mean killing people to take their food I mean killing people to eat them as well.

It was just reported this month of September 2014 that 25% of all the grain produced in America is shipped to China. China knows its middle class population is growing and they like to eat meat. Only thing is they are not very good at producing it (environmental, hygiene, drugs) so reportedly they have bought one of the largest meat producers in this country. They now own that producer of meat made in America and paid (reportedly) 30% over value (god notes) to get it and ensure the people of China will eat. **Paper for tangibles.**

The American government employees (poli-Christian) sat back on their campaign contributions (bribes) and saw nothing wrong with this. But will the American army guard the plants that make this food when it all is being shipped to China? Will Americans be killing Americans to ensure the new middle class of China will eat? For that is what it looks like,,, as I remember those words: *"if you have a sandwich and my kid is hungry,,, I will get that sandwich and my kid will eat."* It's coming!

Killing for water

is next up and this too will cross the globe like wild fire. Glaciers that help cool the planet and give us water to drink are melting at record speed and for countries that rely on them as in South America, these ice giants in some areas are one of their only sources of water, fresh water. They will kill for water and are now killing on a small scale.

The Ganges River in India comes from a glacier that is melting away and when that source is gone this population three times the size of America will be on the move and kill for water. They already are.

Reportedly fifty percent of the rivers in China are polluted and their government, hell bent on building a super power, has paid no attention to the land, air, lakes, streams and rivers. Just get as much paper money **god/notes** as you can and spend it while it still has value. They know the crash of these **god/notes** is coming.

Back home, the Great Lakes are now reported to be lower by about two feet in volume and ports have been complaining that ships can't come into their docks. Think of the square feet of water we are talking about and then think of two feet of that water now gone. How can anyone think the **Super Heating** has not started? What will things be like when the sun's heat raises the temperature by ten degrees across the globe,,, or more? Water will be next to go - right alongside food. They are hand in hand.

If one country has a nice big lake that the indigenous people have been taking care of and another country bordering that country has no water, they will amass on the border and invade, taking the water and the land with it. People will be the only thing in the way. Kill them, eat them, run them off, but get the water at all costs. This will be the future wars along with God. Someone will be there to benefit and make **god/notes.**

Mother Nature will also be in line to take her revenge. For she too, is part of the war on water. In the mid-west we have been pumping water out of the Ogallala Aquifer. That includes eight of the Great Plain states and reportedly in the past 30 to 50 years to make **god/notes** and to grow food for the masses we have been sucking it dry. In that time we have reportedly consumed 50% of that water. The days of abundant, clean water from the Ogallala Aquifer are gone for good. Lakes that sit atop these aquifers could lose their supporting ground and the caverns that open up from sucking out all the water that has been there for thousands of years, will collapse and these lakes will disappear overnight. They are there one minute and will be gone the next. This is not a nightmare I have dreamed up but a real calamity that has happened many times.

Will each state's National Guard be put into service to guard the water resources of that state? Lakes, rivers and streams will be under attack from residents of states that don't have water anymore. Each family will kill to get water and each family will kill to defend their water. This will be across the globe as things just get hotter and hotter. I believe we could be, or are, just one financial crisis away.

Here in Florida we have a large aquifer below us and we are sucking out this water as fast as we can. We have the everglades full of fresh water and the over flow pours into the Gulf of Mexico and the Atlantic Ocean like it had no value. Our thirsty counties near the beaches for the rich, have salty water to drink and they don't like that so they have built large pipes to suck out inland counties' water. One such pipe runs up to a northern county where they now have an alarming amount of sink holes. Let's see, suck water out from beneath our land and then it falls in. Well it must be ok, after all the rich much have their water by the sea,,, right?

I have said how California will be first and it was just reported this month of September 2014 that people in that state for the first time will regulate well drilling. If you have a big farm and you can afford to drill a deep well and pump out the water needed to grow food (make **god/notes**) you will drink. However if you are poor you must now rely on the state (happening today 2014 in California) to bring you water, like India. People's wells are running dry and the days of abundant water are gone. No longer do the farms get water from the glacier or rain, but they stand on the only water there is left. Soon these people will be moving to a neighborhood near you,,, to drink your water. What will you drink when they come?

Global Financial Super Heating

Chapter Ten

One hundred years
and more

Global Financial Super Heating

What will be left depends on governments and how they and their people stand up to **The BIG 3** - oil, the powerful 1%-ers, the warmongers and all god people religions. I believe this **Big 3** will still be with us, dividing us with god and preparing us for invasions from the others that want what we have, for a long time to come. Until a balance happens (resources versus people/all-life) and all people understand the value of each one of our neighbors and we stop killing for God, the coming devastation will continue unabated. Intelligence, to know and to understand, is the nemesis of this power.

One of the true enemies of this slender strip of life we all share is the imaginary gods of the needy and the greedy. Not one god in particular but all gods, new and old are just a weak frightened mind trying to understand a complicated world. We have overcome such ignorance in the past with writing that can be shared, such as $E=MC^2$ came from other people's work brought together by Einstein. Down through the years a mass of information has become available for us all, primarily because of Gutenberg's press and we can once again create beauty from bits of information, before the book burning begins. Remember Germany under Adolf Hitler,,, the good Christian,,, wanting to control people via knowledge and he did. This path to darkness is just before us all.

I believe the population is going to peak in 10 years or sooner, not 150 years like the experts think. This planet is well past its prime and the land cannot grow more food to keep all these people fed. China knew this and created the one child law in 1979 to slow the population growth within their borders. Such laws would have helped other countries like India but it is way too late. I can see one day we will have no choice but to turn in on ourselves for food.

Countries will just buy state of the art drilling platforms that will just drill sideways but instead of going for oil they will suck dry a pristine lake in another country,,, and sell the **Blue Gold** to their people. When you see a dry country or state like Texas suddenly offer lots of water for sale,,, they stole it from someone. This trickery will only postpone the understanding of the great drying of America and the globe.

People have lived in desert regions before and will again, only we will soon have temperatures 20 degrees higher I fear. People will be forced to live in the nights and the few will find **Blue Gold** to drink. The masses will have moved away from the ever growing American desert, long ago. The ones that failed will be nothing more than mummified remains along the high points of the sand and dust covered remaining highways where they ran out of gas or water or both.

Global Financial Super Heating

Rivers and lakes will have dried up and empty cities will dot the country side. There will be towering ghost towns of the past of plenty, with no people, no food, and no water. A few may find a means to cling to these relics of the days of good and plentiful. Like the Scarab Beetles living in the Sahara Desert surviving on the dew that comes in on the rare cool moist nights, then it lives underground during the heat of the day.

This region of America could become an abandoned wasteland where only the insects survive. Anything else will have been eaten long ago. The earth cannot support the masses of people that it once held in its heyday of plenty and the "die off" will be tremendous. We will need to learn to live off bugs for food as one business man in China is doing. He is growing cockroaches in semi trailers and turning them into food for people. He said "it's a growing business."

The surviving populations will move north and south of the equator as the last of the glaciers melts into the sea. All life will be hunted to or near extinction as we crowd closer to the cooler regions of the globe that become tropical. Ireland is now seeing for the first time tropical birds nesting in their country and it is only just starting.

Florida on the other hand may fare better than people think because it is surrounded by water on three sides. We get the evaporating sea water for creating clouds to keep us cool in the heat of the day and rain almost every day of the summer. We may see more rain in this new global heating and I think a time will come when we seal off the underground rivers that dump the **Blue Gold** into the sea. It will become a land bought up by the rich and they will have every piece they can and pass it on to their children. *"**Sell your land or we will kill you and buy it from your kids**."* An island of the well guarded rich, governed by the rich and their descendents from all over the globe. A new master race will emerge as the rest of human life slowly disappears and becomes cheaper and cheaper. The fat lazy children of the rich will be like the ants (Polergus breviceps) that cannot survive without slaves,,, the poor.

Unless all the religious governments get together to save the whole system of life and not just one part or one species, (Jew, Muslim, or Christian) it's going to crash hard. We all know that is not going to happen, so knowledge of their control over us and that we are being controlled, I hope will help. I think it is too late and we who live on this planet will never get together under any of these gods. Why? Because it is just so easy for weak people to rely on their good god to do everything and therefore kill their neighbor that has the wrong god. It is just beyond me to understand. I feel these crusades must stop if the planet is to survive and it is up to us who know and understand to point them out and call them what they are,,, religious crusades. As I write this book and tell Christians of my work even they understand,,, so they are not stupid just ignorant. I tell them it is ok to be spiritual and believe in God if that is what you want, just not these gods or these religions that promote **killing**.

It's not OK!

That might have been a better name for this book.

One way to save life is to control how it is consumed. Unfortunately, we cannot close off the oceans from the commercial exploiters because they belong to the rich countries. Whoever is rich, has the biggest fishing ships; and (the rich) are willing to take it all for themselves, because their god is more powerful, and the right one, of course, and **because they can**; the rich will have all the food.

The oceans have become the toilet of the world and as part of the stewardship of the planet we should and must point out every violation we find. After all, is it not the total sum of all water, that all life shares? The United States has two great dump sites just off the shores of Florida that it has been dumping trash for decades. Not garbage like you and I create but the bad stuff, like mustard gas, that cannot be disposed of cheaply. I am sure there are more than two government dump sites. At the same time Japan is dumping an endless stream of radioactive waste into the food chain system we all rely on.

The need for another system to save and control food is closing on us fast. If we create our own sea, with its own source of food that would be controlled by not-for-profit suppliers, we may have a chance to turn the American desert into a life giving source. That is why I have brought up the Salton City.

If a trench or tunnel were dug connecting Death Valley and the Salton Sea to the Pacific Ocean, we could see a new source of sea life and food source to feed a hungry nation. The stewardship of the planet can only be done if we try to consider all sides of the balance of life. For we only play a small part in a short time here on this globe and we each must learn to bend with the prevailing winds and become like the Willow not the Oak. The true goal for each of us is to not leave a foot print that lasts forever and do so by not trying to own one of everything. After all we don't ever really own anything; we just have the use of it for a short time while here on earth.

Satellites and darkness

If nothing happens and we grow accustomed to the Christian changes that are to come and be forced on the rest of the people of America, as we march backwards in time, one of the unseen destructive forces just above us all will become the loss of satellites and their communications. This will ensure each country will become more isolated and can reinvigorate their religions and this will empower their gods.

The BIG 3 would welcome this because it would end truthful education at your finger tips. Lies regarding history can once more be taught to the young, as those in power can re-write history. No longer would you have current events in one part of the world be known in another part instantaneously.

It will start with one hunk of untracked space debris and at over 1500 MPH it will hit a satellite and destroy it, as it has happened before. This will then create tens of thousands of bits of junk flying at other satellites and BOOM in no time they are gone. One by one this darkness will drape over the land because of our ignorance and the illusiveness of intelligence will slip away. In <u>bare</u> feet, man will stand on the rubble of the past in wonderment and proclaim, *"The gods must have been angry"* - if there is a man left to stand.

Forced to use land lines and the post office to communicate, the weak and needy will fall back on the old reliable, gods. *"The darkness is a sign from God, the end is coming soon,,, just like the good book say."* And the one that is the most religious (and by religious I mean **The BIG 3**, well organized and willing to kill off all life in their god's name) will be the one on top of the pile of dead humanity. How can people not see what is to come and just on the horizon of life?

The old man in the sky will fix it all, so do whatever you want to the land and to the people, then ask for forgiveness and God will let you into his heaven. Now who would want to go to a place like that in the next life, chocked full of ignorant god people? No thanks.

Homosexuality

I still like the American Indian philosophy on this point, *"only Europeans have thrown away people. We welcome all people that contribute to the tribe. We have women warriors and men cooks, all welcomed."* One only need look to the past to see the future and it is right here now in front of us.

The question is, is it better to follow the babblings of a goat herder's teachings of his god or the science that we have today that prove this god crap is so wrong? Each man and each woman provides 23 chromosome pairs to the child we all were and we pass 23 chromosome pairs on to our children. It is there in the balance that there is a mix of male and female that somehow rises to the top. Each one of us cannot help how this mix is to end up. It is not a choice but the genetic growth of the reproductive body in which we reside for a short time.

There is no way we can control the outcome of such reproductive sexual urges, that pull at the mind. But if we try to suppress them or release them, we can find moments of peace and rise above these physical needs for a short time. We all must learn to balance the Yin and Yang energy found within our reproductive physical bodies.

The coming out (if you will) or just acceptance of each person for what they have to offer and can bring to the tribe; I believe is the best way. But you will never convince the frightened, ignorant, goat herder god people of that. From their highest leaders, (those that stand next to god) its ok for their Christian interpreters that teach their god stuff (the holy of the holies) to have sex with little boys. These interpreters (who are also pedophiles) commit violent, homosexual, molestation, acts of rape on helpless children that scar the victims for life and conceal those acts as well as the identities of the perpetrators of those acts. But the Christians claim all homosexual people are bad,,, unless they are preacher men in God's houses having sex with boys – in that case they are just ill.

Christianity has taken over other countries as well as America and one need only look to Russia and their new law this year to end all homosexuality. Just lock them up for 30 years,,, that will make it all go away so the good god people don't have to see or look at it. The part these heartless god people forget is that they (homosexuals) are people too and at one time they (the Christians) were fed to the lions. Persecution is just wrong no matter who is doing it.

Uganda today (2014) is another fine example of the future the Christians have in store for us all. Uganda is reportedly a Christian-run country just full of primarily Roman Catholics, as I understand and they too just don't like these openly gay people. So they have created the **Anti-Homosexuality Act, 2014**, also known as the "**Kill the Gays Bill**" complete with death penalty clauses. It's the Christian left handed people thing all over.

I am sure this is part of the Christian ten commandants of God, stolen from the Jews that states "thou shall not kill",,, except for those non human gays and left handed people. How will they square this with their gods? Does not "shall not kill" mean do not kill?

My mother was taught to be a good God-fearing Christian and she did her best to stop my older brother from writing with his **left** hand. (*Now this is in my lifetime and a true story*) She worked hard to restrain his sick and depraved brain from a future of being a **left**-handed person. He grew up becoming ambidextrous. He also inherited other twisted mental deformities passed on from religious parent to child.

As a child I did not understand why she was so adamant on us kids using our right hand, but now I understand that for thousands of years the goat herder god people think **the devil is left handed**. So they killed all lefties and that is why we live in a right handed world today. I think if the atheists remain quiet there will come a time when lefties will be legally put to death once more, alongside all that speak out or stand against them,,, like atheists.

I now understand why Republicans hate Democrats so much and why they are willing to do anything to destroy them. Some Republicans represent the far RIGHT,,, Christians. Everyone else is the devil and must be destroyed at all costs.

I was spared this trauma as I was born right handed but not spared the other deformities passed on from Christian parents to their children. It is for that reason I chose to NOT have children. I was not given the training as to how to bring up a child properly and I did not want to pass on their sickness to my kids. I therefore try to put down the **parent** and **child** teachings I received as a young person and I try to live in my self-made **adult**. I can only wonder what life would have been like if one of us kids had been born gay, living under these Christian God-fearing masters. Most likely their hacked-up, gay body would have been buried in the basement, all with the loving approval of their Christian god.

Slavery

It is a violation of the Christian God-fearing people to *"covet your neighbor's wife, goods and slaves."* So the goat herding god, sometimes known as a burning bush, is telling these frightened people, it is ok to have slaves. *Now isn't that nice?*

Yet Christians did not invent slavery; remember that the ten commandants of God were stolen from the Jews. Slavery goes back far before the Jews and most likely can be traced back to someone that tied a vine around another's neck to keep them in bondage. As long as they are stronger they have the right,,, **because they can** and now God gives them the right.

Perhaps the frightened goat herder god people got the idea from the ants. *Poliergus breviceps* is a type of ant parasite that has lost the ability to care for not only itself but its young. It cannot hunt for food, feed its young or queen or clean up its waste. So they enslave other ants to do this work for them as they live a life of luxury. *Sound familiar?* It does start to make sense that there is a parasite people found within the human nest of life. These Poliergus breviceps people or PB-People, when one starts to look closely, resemble the one percent-ers. It may just be part of our genetic makeup, like gays, to grow into men and women and in-between. Then these PB-People enslave others to do their work, living off the weaker ones, as do all highly religious people, the teachers of God, within all towers (cathedrals, mosques, temples, etc.) to the gods. They truly are,,, all PB-People for they can't care for themselves.

China: reportedly this country is now made up of many warring provinces and would enslave captured prisoners. They would help build the longest grave yard in the world. At one time the current Great Wall of China was many walls that

over time became one and if you were a slave working on this wall and you became ill, they would just bury you were you dropped. You are intended to remain nameless and forgotten, just crushed bones under the stones and today under the feet of the smiling uneducated ignorant tourist. You must be very sick indeed to want to go to such a place and un-respectfully tread on the unnamed dead.

This country has always put higher value on male babies over female babies. The boy baby would help the father work the land but a female baby had little or no value. I remember hearing of the **Baby Wall** where women would take their unwanted female babies and toss them over this wall to get rid of them. This created a shortage of good breeding females and China would buy slave girls from pirates that trolled the Korean waters.

This was banned in the late 600s but it had little or no effect on the business of slavery, so it just went underground, like today across the world. Records indicate this practice continued up to and after WWII. Then came the one Child Law and once more female babies were aborted for the male babies and a shortage was created even stronger and to this day eligible bachelors must be rich to attract a female to his nest. Or buy a young female from Vietnam, tricked into coming to China looking for a high paying job. The kidnapped Vietnam girls have two choices, one, get married or two, work in the brothels. The one good thing is when the Chinese government finds these girls they kick them out of China,,, unlike Christian America.

In America we take illegal foreigners to the bus station and send them anywhere in the United States they want to go. That is our immigration law. Free food, free housing, free child care, free health care, free schooling, free prisons and all at the expense of the states,,, not the federal government. We who have lived here all our lives, paid our taxes and helped build this country give them a free ride. Some think this immigration policy or lack thereof, is only to increase the tax base for the federal government by creating new Americans via new babies born to foreigners, paid for by each state,,, our money. Could the **BIG 3** be behind such a lack of policy? Stop and think, who does such a lack of policy benefit?

Islamic/Muslim: also take part in this slave business and allegedly enslaved Christians to work their slave ships. But they also sold salves to the Americans, mostly men and the majority of the female slaves went to the Middle East, part of the Arab slave trade.

The male slaves did not fend well under this group of slave traders and allegedly most died in transport. The female slaves sent to the Middle East did not fare much better and reportedly around 80% would die on the trip there. When they would bring forth a child it was most likely killed on the spot.

However, to Christian American slave traders,,, the new child was just more money.

The Islamic slavery laws are covered in great length in their holy (god) books. *Isn't that nice?* Seems slavery is an acceptable condition that could be done under limited circumstances to this day, if I understand it correctly.

However unlike Christians and Jews, one of the five pillars of Islam is to donate money to free slaves in countries where slavery exists, in hopes that slavery will cease to exist in that country. I don't think they have that much money, based on the growing sex slave trade of today.

Jew: also have lots of laws on how to treat their slaves. Allegedly their Hebrew bible (god book) has two sets of laws covering this point: One for Canaanite slaves and one more lenient for Hebrew slaves. *Now isn't that special that they separate them?*

In these more modern times, under the world's scrutiny, supporters of slavery use these religious laws to provide their religious justification for slavery. God says it's ok,,, however today the idea of ownership of a slave by a human (in Judaism) is absolutely unacceptable. But I noticed they did not say anything about corporations owning slaves.

However Jews are extra special people (are not all the god people?) that have some birth right to heaven and all things non-Jewish are given to them by **their** god. All non-Jewish people are called Goyim and I, as a Goy, have next to no value. I, the Goy, would be rated as nothing more than cattle,,, if that high. This is their word and their interpretation, as I understand.

As one of the herd of Goyim I am glad to say, I will not be going to their heaven. Why would you want to spend eternity with such evil heartless people,,, serving their god? Just look how the Jewish occupiers treat the people in Palestine. The invading Jews kill the resisting Islamic people and drive over their houses with tanks, given to them by Christian Americans. All Americans are collaborators in their murders and once more,,, that is ok with this Christian government because Christians are killing Muslims via the Jews - *"Enemies of my enemies killing each other."* To this day even Germany stands behind the Jews that have stolen the Palestine land, enriched themselves, and now kill the Palestine people who try to take back what the Jews took and the Christians helped with their support. There will never be peace until all Jews return the stolen land. Right is right and these killing, land stealing Jews are wrong and it is wrong for Christian America to support them.

Swedish slaves: oh yes they too were in the slave business in their history at the beginning and had a free port in the Caribbean. The king charged an export tax on all slaves from their invaded Caribbean island and sold high quality iron for chains for the slaves.

Around the 1850s Sweden and its colonies (islands stolen) abolished slavery. But today allegedly they participate in the sex slave industry on a small scale, as do most all countries.

Today: slavery is a growing business and as Christian rule grows over this land presently called America, so will the slave trade re-emerge ever stronger. Christians will get past this little bump in the road of life regarding decency, morality and humanity and once more can enjoy their God given right to have slaves. *Now don't be jealous,,, for God wont like that.*

It was about ten years ago that it was reported (leaked) the CIA estimated America had a healthy and growing slave trade. Yes in America,,, women and children brought to this country as slave labor and prostitutes in numbers totaling over 50,000 per year. Today I would bet that number has more than doubled - all under the loving eyes of all the good Christians, helping to grow the tax base.

The number of calls to sex trade crisis help lines has reportedly grown 600% from 2008 to 2013. So it appears that under hard times the good Christians need more slaves or people just get a lot cheaper.

Global Financial Super Heating

This is something we Goyim must get used to as Christians march us backwards in time and modern slavery becomes the norm. As country by country and state by state becomes Christian ruled and the courts impose the old bible on all of us, look for the *erection* of crosses to be used in front of the court house next to the poles for impaling the defiant ones and the slave auction blocks set between. Witches and warlocks as well as the atheists will burn on the courthouse steps,,, all part of the gods' loving plans.

Global slavery: the estimates are all over the board while we all pretend slavery is not in our back yard. After all, the god people would not want these numbers known or leaked out to the press,,, it's **embarrassing**. You have to remember, it has only been a short time that this slavery thing has been a **not nice thing to do or talk about**. So they have to hide it like the pedophiles under the Christian leadership (the pope). They don't want to talk about that either,,, just keep sending the church money.

Uganda: and they now have come full circle and once more rising to the top, this good Christian country that has instilled the **Kill a Gay Law**, also has slavery. (*Go figure!*) Allegedly women and children are sold in cattle market style and shipped all over the world. I am sure some of those countries that receive these slaves are also good Christian led governments as well, so that makes it all ok. ***Per God,,, it's fine.***

As the dollar shrinks in value across the globe and food becomes scarcer, the one thing we have too much of,,, is people. So slavery will become a new old business and this small bump of humanity in the road of life, will be short lived and once more we can sell our children into slavery like the good old days. Pretty blond female children will bring a premium.

World Prison Population

Every time I think I have seen it all,,, there seems to be one more thing. The numbers are staggering when you look at countries incarceration rate around the world VS their religion. Yes it would seem, religion and that God to that religion of that country, affects the kindness and forgiving aspects of their government and their people.

The numbers vary from report to report and are not available from some countries, so from the ones I could find I have created an average to point out the prison population per 100,000 people in that country from mutable reports.

It should be noted that these are estimates only and are sometimes loosely based on thin or light information that I have found to help me with these numbers and conclusions I have drawn.

Turkey.....Islam

Perhaps because of Sharia/Muslim Law and their Islamic punishments, the incarceration rate is low in Turkey. I estimate it is just under or at 0.09% out of every 100,000 people. Of course I do not have the best of information and these numbers could be wrong but it may be that when people are stoned to death or have their heads chopped off in the public square for adultery or their hands cut off for stealing, it is a good deterrent for crime and that is why the numbers are so low.

So it could be a harsh and struck god lowers prison population or that their god said women must cover their heads and some wear a burqa, that may help keep crime low. Or that Islamic man is made in God's image, so he is free from this covering requirement and is a little god himself, so the law is perhaps more flexible. However it happens, Sharia/Muslim Law has the lowest incarceration rate that I can find.

China..... Communist Party
An Atheist organization

These people are ruled with an iron fist under their dictatorship masters, as we in Christian America are taught and yet prison populations are allegedly low. It was reported that they do execute a lot of people (dissenting voices like mine, as I understand) every year so they can hang on to the power or they do it **because they can**. Regardless of how or why, the prison population works out to about 00.12% per 100,000 of this communist atheist organization.

However you cut it, China has been kicking our ass in the business world and even with the financial disaster of 2007 they did just fine. They own us via all the bonds they have bought and have lifted their countries up from the dark ages to a super global power in just a few years. They still take care of their people and do so without god.

One of the only drawbacks they face is the same one we all face and that is the crash of the dollar. They have spent the green back as quick as they could because, I believe, they know it is crashing, so better to turn it into infrastructure and new cities than keep it in the bank and watch it drop in value. They have exchanged our paper **god/notes** for real property, real things. Real smart!

The value of this infrastructure and real estate is considered to be a big financial bubble on the brink of popping. Like the shark market the value of properties is well over inflated. But when the crash happens they will own something real and the rest of us will have a pile of green paper or **god/notes**. Who will be better off? Without god they have built a super power that out paces Christian America and they are buying this country and its people. Just look to congress for these traders.

England.....Christian

Now we get up to the first of the Christian led countries. The next in my line and the lowest in the god ranking of Christianity, seems to go to England. Their percent of the population works out to be just about 00.15% of each 100,000 people.

As Christians go this is by far the best and I attribute these low numbers to three factors.

1) Their education system far surpasses ours hear in Christian America.

2) The free health care system that has been in effect since 1946 offers doctor supervised drug addiction assistance for its entire population. They don't have to steal to buy drugs and help is right there for all.

3) Abortion is widely accepted and used to prevent the growth of a population of unwanted abandoned street children that grow up to be criminals filling up their prisons.

Russia.....Christian

There is a large jump in the number of people in the Christian Russian government prisons and within the population of each 100,000 people I found just over 00.60%. Once more I can't say how accurate these numbers are but I will bet they will change and start to grow as Putin starts to lock up all the gays under his new anti gay laws.

It should be noted that Russia at one time had no less than twenty concentration camps and enslaved and murdered hundreds of thousands (some records indicate this number could be in the millions) of its own people. There is no telling if these camps are still working or soon will hold homosexuals and others that may speak up like Muslims, Jews and atheists.

I envision political prisoners will start to grow as they are in America, only I can see a day when Vladimir Putin, a good Christian himself, starts to lock up all the Muslims and atheists. Next I can see he will send the Jews to the work camps with a one way ticket and we will never see them or hear from them again. Looks like it is all part of this master Christian God's plan, covering the globe, unfolding before our silent eyes. Silent until the day those in power, doing God's work, come for us. *Now it is a problem and it is not right*!

Christian America
Feel the love

Sadly I must tell you that this country of the free and the brave has the worst record in the world for the incarceration of its people. The rate is at or near 00.70% (of the population reported as incarcerated) and it is not hard to see why, when one looks at how this loving and forgiving Christian government pursues its murdering heartless agenda. These numbers do not include people held in prison without a trial or convicted in secret courts and sent to secret prisons or held overseas in Christian American run torture dungeons. *Can't you just feel the love?*

I see **five** factors that contribute to these numbers rising over the past 40 years and we should look in depth at them so as to understand. Before WWII if you were '**not right**' you could find yourself in the Looney Bin or the Nut House. Harsh names given to mental hospitals but it is a hard fact that a federally run hospital was better than leaving these poor people on the street to harm themselves or others.

After WWII we had electric shock and in or about the early 50s the practice of treatment for the mentally ill included the new surgery called lobotomy. Discovered in the 1890s to control a dogs aggressive behavior it was widely used in America to control people in mental institutions. At that time there were no drugs to help people and this was seen by some as the best or only help available.

At the end of the 50s and the beginning of the 60s records show medication was able to help the mentally ill and the numbers started to drop. This decline continued as the federal government's leaders saw such dollars spent to help the mentally ill as a poor investment and a reduction of funding for <u>social welfare</u> became the far right's Christian agenda. *Really can't you just feel the love?*

The ever growing need to get these people off welfare and off the federal government's payroll continued as did better and better medication. Then a truly malleable president, Ronald Reagan was elected and the demands of the big business community (**The BIG 3**) were met as these mental hospitals were closed in the 80s so America could spend <u>that</u> money,,, to spread Christian values in wars across the globe and get the oil, kill Muslims, and set up the Jews for the kill. *And we still say nothing.*

Without regard for the well-being of the mentally ill, Reagan's financial goals, or voodoo economics, were to remain with us to this very day. Literally these mental hospitals opened their doors, handed the mentally ill people in their care a bottle of pills, and pushed them out, locking the doors behind them. The cost of care transferred from the federal government to the states.

These mentally ill people did not take their pills, (go figure) were homeless, and committed crimes to feed themselves and ended up going to state prisons. The spike of prison and jail populations grew and only now is starting to level off.

Global Financial Super Heating

Many people believe our prison populations in America are the **highest in the world** for the following reasons:

1) The heartless acts of Ronald Reagan, a Presbyterian baptized for Christ (the war industry now had the money to kill people (Muslims) while spreading the word of this Christian god) and the states had to foot the bills for the mentally ill.

2) The acts of the Christian lawmakers in Washington, the Poli-Christians, that enacted mandatory sentences for crimes. Per these Christian lawmakers we don't need judges to show acts of Christian kindness or mercy to the people - just send them to state prison. Let the states pay for federally mandated laws and Christian punishment. *So much for a loving forgiving god.*

3) The war on drugs declared by Richard Milhous Nixon, a Quaker (Christian), is good for business, good for private prisons but bad for people. It has enriched the drug dealers and help the gun industry, but has left these people (like the mentally ill) to fend for themselves (more throw-away people). The war on drugs has only helped to divide us as a people and to see this we need only look at other developed countries that are not over run by the heartless Christian love that pretends to do good.

4) Private prisons that have but one goal - make money in the business of warehousing people. The last thing they want is to parole people or have an empty bed. They are like a hotel; they want all the beds full so they can make all the money. The war on drugs and dumping the mentally ill on the states is good for big business.

5) The last reason is immigration. Our laws for immigration are simple, just get to America and we will provide you with a bus ticket to any place you want to go. You can get free food, a free home and free health care for you and your kids – and free prison.

Sign me up I want to go.

The influx of unwanted, undocumented, and uneducated people with low morals and poor hygiene (never saw toilet paper before) is too great. These unwelcome neighbors are now living next door to you, stealing your hubcaps, and killing your dog for food, while throwing their trash out the front door into the yard for all to see. This is how a Christian government is run - we must save all the people we can. It is part of God's plan, breed like rabbits and let someone else pay for the cost. *I am willing to bet, if the Christian church had to pay for all these unwanted babies, they would embrace abortion. Their love of money is too strong. Just look how they at the top live,,, like kings.*

Israel prisons....Jew

Global Financial Super Heating

Israel is a new and unusual country bought and paid for with American Christian dollars. The information I could find about it was slim, at best. However, it looks like 00.25% of the population is behind bars. Only this is an occupied country and I am willing to bet these numbers don't include political prisoners or the indigenous people of Palestine held in death camps.

This war tormented area is never going to be at peace and the Jews can build all the walls they want but I feel some day they will come crashing down on them. This little patch of arid land has value because of,,, you guessed it,,, God.

It seems that all three religions want to own this magical mystical land of fairies, magic stardust, magic rivers and streams, and yes, one magic brick wall (*can't forget that*). So far the Christians have been winning and using the Jews to maintain their Christian claims to this so called holy land. *To some of us, holy stands for hell on earth.*

There have been so many wars over this part of God's land and it looks like it started long before Jesus Christ was born. But now that he has come and gone this place has even more value. Allegedly, with the need to own this plot of land, the 'thou shall not kill' people, Roman Christians, started the first conflict with Islam on or about 1096 and did their best to kill all the Muslims that stood in their way, **defending** their land, as anyone would. Seems the good Christians have invaded this Arab and Islamic/Muslim land many times.

Global Financial Super Heating

If I have it right, the British Christians invaded this land many times as well - 1840, 1917 and in 1922 they were awarded a mandate of some type (most likely from the Christian church or court, same thing) giving them some right to be there *(the power of the pen)*. Slowly the Jews started to migrate to this land hoping to start a Jewish state. Arabs and Palestinians revolted in 1936 but Britain, or the Christians, stopped them. This hate and the Arab-Jewish tensions continued to grow as the Jewish massive migration from Europe and Muslim countries led to more conflicts.

In 1947 the British Government proclaimed their desire to end the mandate and the United Nations General Assembly voted to partition the territory. Reportedly Israeli independence in 1948 saw over 700,000 Palestinians flee or driven from their homes and unable to return following the Lausanne Conference of 1949.

So the Jews were murdered, persecuted and driven out of Germany (their home land) by the evil heartless Nazis (Christians) leaving their homes behind with no compensation and now the Arabs and Palestinian people were murdered, persecuted and driven out of their homes by the evil heartless Jewish Nazis (backed with Christian dollars) and given no compensation.

The following four maps show how both countries with the Christian church behind them, under a British mandate and under a French mandate, divide up this part of the world. *Today*

(2014) for some of us it is American Christian money doing all the killing.

If these maps are correct and I say correct because maps are always being re-drawn by one power over another, Palestine was a big country. Now stop and look at the first map #1(Page 213) for a moment and think what life must be like for the descendants of this once great country.

Put yourself in their place. You are a small child sitting at the dinner table when your older brother, your dad, your grandfather and your great grandfather are somehow still alive and all speak on how their land was stolen by the Jews. The Jews get the money and arms from the American Christians to kill your people. *Now you must share the same feelings the indigenous people of this land called America must have,,, the native American Indians. The parallels are striking and sickening.*

A nation made up of tribes of people murdered defending their land from an invading force. They claim it to this day, **"America was founded on good Christian beliefs."** They called them savages then, they call them terrorists today, helping justify their Christian actions of murder and aggression.

If you doubt this for any reason, look at a map of the United States of America and try to find the last bits of land, granted by the invaders, to the indigenous people of this country. Somehow the good Christians did not kill them all. You may need a magnifying glass to find those tiny spots on the maps of America.

Now compare the map of America with its Christian granted reservations for the indigenous people of this country, to map #4 (Page 213) of what is left of Palestine. Do you not see a similarity and pattern to Christians murdering aggression?

Utter and total annihilation of a people for their land is **genocide** and we all look the other way and say nothing while it happens today, 2014, before our eyes. This is also happening in Tibet and other countries as we remain silent. It must be OK to kill them, destroy their heritage and take their land for they are not Christian. As long as people that are not Christian are being murdered,,, it's OK.

For me I will say it, **Christians are aiding and abetting Jews in genocide against the Palestine people, "occupied terrorist"**.

The four maps on page 213 will help show what happens when a religion wants and can take land from another race of people and justify their actions by dehumanizing that race of people.

Whatever you have been told,,, in the past 100 years a country has fallen off the face of the earth and no one seems to care except the people being murdered. There is a word for this and it is

Genocide!

It should be noted that the world is carved up all the time by **people that do it because they can** while the rest of us sit back,,, say and do nothing.

Wrong is wrong!
And murder is murder!

1. **Map one** shows the country of Palestine in all its greatness before Christian and Jewish interventions or genocide about or before 1897 and before the world Zionist organization founded and established a home for Jewish people.
2. **Map two** shows the country of Palestine cut down to 1/3 of its former greatness in 1917 under the declaration from the United Kingdom's Foreign Secretary,,, finally creating a home for the Jews on someone else's land. With the British mandate of 1922 and the French Mandate of 1923 falling in line. *Was this done just to get the Jews out of their countries?*
3. **Map three** is after WWII and the Partition Plan of 1947. Christian America was stepping in.
4. **Map four** reveals for us all to see the full effects of Christian and Jewish genocide under **The BIG 3**.

All dates and times are subject to the best information I could find. I did not divide up these countries so I don't know what they looked like before this genocide began.

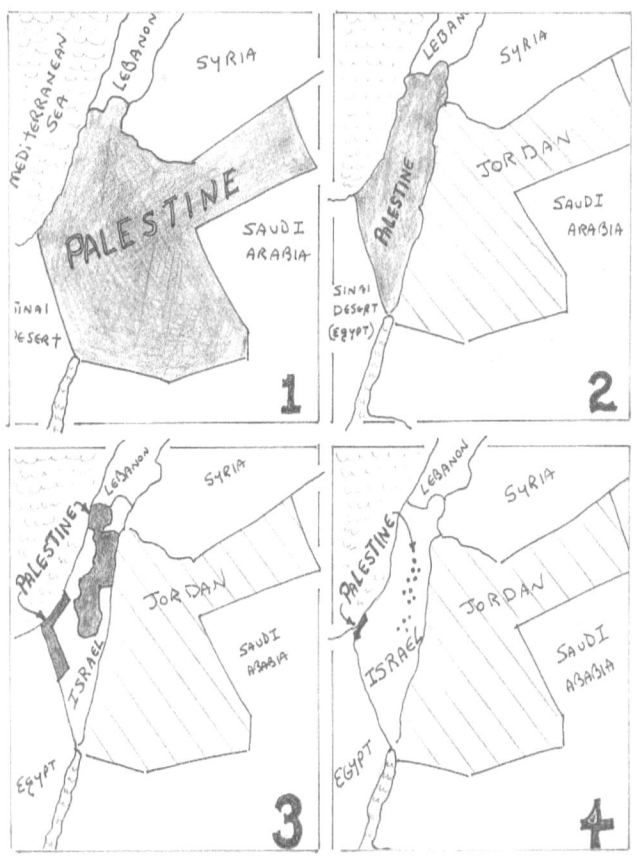

The numbers are always fun to look at and help point to the truth. Israel is made up of 8,000,000 people and their GDP is close to 300 billion dollars. Now these numbers may or may not include dollars and people via occupation (stolen farm land).

Now the war industry in Israel gets a free gift of 3 billion dollars from the Christian American government to spend on its ongoing wars (Muslim land grab) to help the Jews keep the occupied land and the Christians get to have access to their gods birth place. *(To keep the record straight, this is the bastard executed criminal Jew man-god.)* The Jews get their Jewish state *(stained with Palestine Arab Muslim blood)* and the Christians pay for it with our tax money.

Now remember I said there were 8 million people in Israel and they get 3 billion dollars per year as a gift from Christian America. That is 375 dollars for each man, woman and child in that country, every year. And just who do you think is authorizing this payment for their (the Jews) free ride,,, **The BIG 3**?

The Israeli Commissioner of Prisons oversees 33 correctional facilities. Of those prisoners reportedly about 60% are convicted of a real crime and the remaining prisoners are there for **security** offenses. My guess is those are the Palestinian people that wanted their stolen land back from the Jews, paid for by the Christians.

Global Financial Super Heating

With this religious history and the occupiers of this land I too could see how I would join the fight to get them out of my country and off my land. Today, June 2014, it was reported the Jews are again, indiscriminately bombing the Palestinian people and killing women, children, and men that have nothing to do with this. It looks as though the Jews are nothing more than high paid terrorists - front men for the criminal Christian organization that has taken over America and funds the occupation of this land so Christians can have access to their god's birth place. *Now that must be a sin.* *What type of god would want this?*

One passing note: the Israeli Supreme Court struck down the plans for a private prison and determined it to be **unconstitutional and a violation of human rights**. Unlike Christians or poli-Christians that will do anything to make rich corporations even richer, regardless of how people are treated (in private prisons for profit) just as long as they (poli-Christians) are given bribes (I mean campaign contributions) and they can be reelected.

Global Financial Super Heating

Chapter Eleven

Solutions?

Global Financial Super Heating

Looking over the time line of religion we are limited as to records and the best I can find when man first created God, started around the 34th century BC. Now I have <u>not</u> made religion a lifetime study or quest to know all there is to know about these gods of the past,,, because I don't care. I often mix up priest and rabbi for fun to see holy people's surprising reactions.

"I see you are a Christian, so how is the rabbi doing?" "I am not Jewish!" "Well you believe in the king of Jews,,, Jesus don't you? That makes you a Jew." Their deer in the headlights look is priceless.

All those other poor gods are only part of the dust of life and are gone for good (we hope). But then we discovered writing and we could save the lunatic words of the greedy over the needy (PB people) and pass them on to the next generation, these gods reappeared and remain with us today.

Global Financial Super Heating

I remember seeing a vessel that reportedly showed the Chakra system of the human body dating over 6,500 years ago. Chakras are part of the subtle body not part of the physical body. Today this is part of Yoga that dates back around 5,000 years and Buddhism that is about 2,500 years old.

Modern Judaism is said to be about 4,000 years old and as I recall its roots are found about 4,500 years ago in the chakra system whereby the high priest must wear a harness to keep their left hand over the heart chakra. It's my understanding that this harness keeps the mind focused on the love in the heart. Apparently they needed help back then as well as today to remember to be kind to people and show love. I think most religious people today could use one of these harnesses. But the left hand,,, that's Satan,,, right? Is that where the left handed thing started?

Then reportedly Islam came on the scene about 600 a.d. and like the Christians there are several types. From the news today it seems each type is trying to kill off the other and have been warring like the Protestants and the other Christians for over a thousand years.

Today it looks like the good Christians try to help make peace by selling war supplies to all sides of Islam. Seems Christians can't help the Muslim kill each other fast enough. If you paid attention to the last meeting between Vladimir Putin and Barack Obama on September 6th 2013, it looked to some of us like they made a pact with each other and have agreed to give all warring Muslims a place to fight and kill each other,,, Syria. It looks like the Christian **solution** to Islam. Both Putin and Obama are good Christians and this could be how they spread their Christian love.

A good Christian

A Russian Orthodox
Christian

September 6, 2013
Could this be what they really said?

"Hear is the deal,,, I will supply Syria on the east with small arms and you supply small arms to the whoever is on the west. Let our enemies kill our enemies and let the newest Christian crusades continue."

"Done! We did it in Palestine, Afghanistan, Iraq Pakistan and Libya,,, what's one more. I will add Syria to our save-yours list of conquests. Our lord will have a very special place for us in heaven.

William J. Ryan ©2014 #094

Know thy Enemy

The **US Army's** *(some call a branch of the Christian killing machine)* ranking system is the first I want to look at. It is very complicated and comes with Grades, Insignias, and Titles *(oh boy)*. Their system starts with private, private 2, private first class, specialist, corporal, sergeant, staff sergeant, sergeant first class, master sergeant, first sergeant, sergeant major, command sergeant major, sergeant major of the army, warrant officer, chief warrant officer 2, chief warrant officer 3, chief warrant officer 4, chief warrant officer 5, second lieutenant, first lieutenant, captain, major, lieutenant colonel, colonel, brigadier general, major general, lieutenant general, general and finally,,, general of the army.

Wow!!! I guess you need that many titles if you're going to fight wars all over the globe and be the policemen of the world. Or it is needed to defend **American** business **Interests**.

Now let's look at the **ranks of the catholic clergy**. It like the army starts with the lowest, those Christian soldiers. The laity, (people baptized as Catholics) deacons are next, then priest, monsignor, bishop, archbishop, cardinal then and finally the pope, highest of the highs standing next to their god.

Not as complicated as the US Army but for an antiquated warring cult, hell bent on global domination, willing to kill those that stand in their way and take their conquered properties, it seems to work well for them. It's a good system of domination or terrorist organization,,, if you like those types of things.

The next one I would like to explore is the **Native American Indian system of ranking**. Reportedly there are over 800 tribes in the new land of Columbus,,, no, wait, the king did not like him so they called it America. Theirs is a simpler system if I understand it and I did not check them all. In no order we have the Chief-leaders, then the War Chiefs, Holy men, Holy women, Warriors, Gatherers, Hunters and Elders that are highly respected.

I remember hearing the words of the last War Chief, as he explained there were several steps to get that title and one was, *"to become a War chief one must steal an enemy's horse in a time of war"* and in WWII he did such a thing in Germany. Apparently he was the last to gain such a title and there will be no more Native American Indian War Chiefs. This must make all American Christians very happy for the voices of the indigenous people of this land will become silent for all time. Only people like myself remembering what the good Christians did to those people, driving them out of their lands to the worst the country had to offer, to die. Just like the Jew/Christians are doing in Israel today to the Palestinian people. I remember hearing one say, "drive them into the sea until they are all dead and silent." *These are words of people of faith,,, god people.*

Jewish system of ranking,,, who cares! When you look at how the Jewish people treat the Palestinian people one can clearly see there is no god. From what I can find there are no less than two types of this religion, Hasidic Judaism and Orthodox Judaism, if I have it right. Regardless, it is my understanding that only Jewish people are going to heaven and the rest of us are Goyim, (goats and cows). Where is their **piety** or loving-kindness? Maybe it's for the Jewish people only.

Atheist system of ranking,,, NONE that I know of. I propose an atheist ranking system like what I understand the Gila River Indian Community has, whereby the leader is **selected** not elected. A system of drafting an individual into a slot for leadership of all atheists for a selected time or until their leadership comes into question. He or she is chosen by all in the tribe to have the qualities they want as a leader. If the candidates try too hard to be elected via their kind acts to others, they are proven to be phony (poli-Christian) and passed over for leadership. You see it must be sincere qualities they require for guidance of the whole tribe, all people.

If the atheists formed such a system of selection for their leaders I could think of no greater honor that could be bestowed on a human. No one person could do it all so this person would need generals of some type to help them, for the weight of the world would be on those chosen persons' shoulders. All of us would turn to them for leadership and guidance as to how to expose and overcome the ignorance and damage of gods and greed. Their life as they once knew it would be over for now they must lead, for they have been chosen. They must find a way to reveal the truth.

Such persons to be given such a position of honor would become like the people of the Greatest Generation and the men that were known as the $1.00 per year men. They worked to overcome the German Christian leader that was crossing the globe, working for his Christian Gods. Killing the Jews was a vengeful act of Christians, for as I said, they believe the Jews kill their man-god Christ. It's called **Jewish Deicide** and is the belief, that all the Jews are responsible for killing their man-god Christ.

As part of the New Testament (*the 2nd or 3rd or 4th re-write of their holy book*) (*re-writes help clean up the silly parts - apparently they missed a few*) responsibility for God's death (*God is dead,,, now I know why the god people kill so much,,, he is dead!*) is Jewish (*no Christians at that time,,, thank God*) and the Jewish authorities in Roman Judea charged Jesus with blasphemy, however Christians believe Jews did not have the authority to have God/Jesus put to death. Now we understand why the Christians want to kill the Jews. Reportedly under the loving guidance of the Roman Catholic Church, it was summarized for us in 1962 to 1965 and the pope just full of God's love and forgiveness established "Christ-Killer" as part of the Jewish deicide. Is this the license to kill that the Christians needed from the start and now have? Not that they need any license to kill, just the want of your land is sufficient cause for genocide. Hitler understood.

Justification for genocide makes for good bedtime reading and is always fun to read to your children on Sunday morning filling them with the magic of hate, division and separation, turning them into the next generation of murderers,,, all with God's love behind them.

A litany of thou shalt not's

It was just reported on the news, 5-31-14 that a catholic school in America has their teachers sign a **contract** referred to as some type of **morality clause**. I obtained several different forms of what I believe to be copies of these **minister teacher contracts** used by this and other (some call them) Christian cults. It is believed by some that the minister teachers are to control and thereby **brainwash children** with their hate and justification of genocide for their god. These contracts are full of legalese and speak of all the dos and don'ts with **doctrines of morals**. *Funny words coming from Christians don't you think?*

Some refer to the signee as Principal-Minister and throughout the contract they are the Teacher-Minister. It uses such holy words as *"catholic principles, lifestyles"* and **"by word and example reflects religious values"**.

But nowhere did it say thou shall not have sex with little boys, and if you do or know of others that have, report it to the police immediately. It must not be part of the Christian religious value system that they so highly speak of. So sex/rape and pedophilia and knowledge of same are ok as long as it is covered up and hidden from the outside public. This teaching has now bled into the public school system (as I understand) for they as well are covering up sex crimes across the Christian land of America. They must get that from the top.

It was then that it occurred to me that there is a way to bring the evil that is in this god out into the light for all to see. I have narrowed down a few of the weak points that make up the pillars of this strange religion or cult and it is my suggestion to offer them as a platform for atheists (truth tellers) to build upon.

Because words have sometimes multiple and confusing meaning I felt the need to offer definitions to the following words so atheists can more clearly see the value of words and their power. Sometimes boiling down the muck of life will bring revelations. Plus these words are keys to the next chapter and understanding just how I believe we could move forward. The power of knowledge will set us free to end the death grip hold over us all by the **BIG 3**.

The Achilles Heel

The **Achilles** tendon is one of the longest tendons in the human body starting at the heel of your foot and running up to your calf muscles. When damaged, it can bring down the strongest of men.

Greek mythology records report **Achilles** the person, as a baby, was dipped in the **magical** river of Styx, but mom held on to his foot and the **magic** water did not rinse over his heel and when he was a man he was shot in that heel, with a poisonous arrow and it killed him. I wonder how many people today believe in this **magic** river of silliness.

Cult

Cult is from the Latin word for worship. It is a group of people or an organization comprised of deviant religious practices. Such as, but not limited to, **eating of human flesh**, **drinking of human blood** and dipping a new born in **magic** water, blessed from a deity, would be considered by some,,, as deviant. This should extend to incorporating the young into the doctrine of the group via brainwashing in Sunday school and having sex with little boys and covering it up and hiding it from the law of free non brain washed people.

Reportedly the Christians are the strongest endorsers of this term **cult** and to label any other religion that does not fall in line with their deities is the goal, delegitimizing them (**terrorist**). Therefore it is my understanding of this word **cult**, which should include all mainstream Jew, Muslims, Christians and Christianity because they fully meet these requirements *(by their own Christian descriptions)* and would be a **cult**.

Terrorism

This term is an overly used word to describe anyone that disagrees with the **majority or people in power,** *(like the BIG 3)*. The dissenters' voices *(like mine)* are easily labeled with this term and to date there are reportedly over a hundred different meanings.

It seems to depend on which side of the fence you are sitting on, as to who is the **terrorist**. America's leaders ordered an invasion of a country that (from the view point of some) did nothing to us except be Muslim and have oil. America called them (the deceived and misled invaders) Freedom Fighters. The families left alive in Iraq after the Freedom Fighters had killed their loved ones, called Americans **invaders**, **occupiers** and **terrorists**. This term (terrorism) has also been linked to unlawful tactics by criminal organizations and racketeers to enforce a code of silence. But that describes the leaders of Israel, England, Russia and America (to name but a few) making all Jews and all Christians out to be **terrorists** (some think).

Crusades

A military campaign endorsed by the Roman Catholic Church under pope urban II, who allegedly started the first Christian **crusade** to kill Muslims and take their land in or about 1095. It has been claimed that this **crusade** was to stop the expansion of Islam and gain access to land near Jerusalem. Regardless of the reasons, this appears to outsiders as though Christians are invaders and this is clearly an act of terrorism and genocide.

I am not a scholar of religion and I don't want to be, but I can find a total of only five **crusades** (I am sure there are more) that have been reported in the European/Middle East. And yet there is nothing noted as to the **crusades** in the Americas, north and south let alone Nazi Germany, the Korean and the Vietnam expansions of Christianity and today its Iraq, Iran, Pakistan, Palestine, and Afghanistan.

Today we sit back and wonder what is going on and why are we fighting all over the world and I offer this: it is just another Christian **crusade, on multiple fronts,** as an explanation of their god is forced on more people, so they (the ignorant) can be controlled. The underlying goal is the same as it has been for over a thousand years, kill Muslims, take their land and kill the Jews that killed their god. Christianity and other religions of gods are never going to change unless non-followers show them for what they <u>truly</u> are,,, murderers, pedophiles, cults, terrorists, invaders and occupiers. All this genocide is for money and God.

Each religion seems to have these qualities of terrorism and at some point erects walls to keep out the evil non-believers. People that suffer from **scrupulosity** must have others to lean on for they are sick and weak. It would appear that the concept of God comes with walls to divide us as people leading to wars. Sounds more like the devil,,, no God to me.

Abstinence

Another code of the church is the **law of chastity** and it is required that abstinence from sex before marriage be observed. And yet pedophiles within the church do not observe this law as well as other laws like the, **thou shall not kill** thing.

In March of this year 2014 it was reported that a cardinal from the Christian church said, **(and I am not making this up)** *'pedophilia is a psychological illness and not a criminal condition'*. WOW!!! Is there anyone of you that is not sickened by those words? What kind of a twisted mind must a person have to believe such a thing? Clearly they have no empathy for the raped child whose life is ruined by a criminal <u>**rape-priest**</u> pedophile.

This cardinal's position or stance, is to some a soulless act, done only to protect the guilty and the good name (if this cult can have a good name) of the church they represent. I can almost can smell the sulfur and I wonder how deep does this evil run? Oh yeah, there is one more thing, this cardinal reportedly was and is a supporter of the current pope and helped him get his job while helping to protect pedophiles.

This helps to explain why the pope is not releasing to law enforcement the names of the pedophiles dismissed within the church - *as any decent person would do.* To the Christian church the rape of children, is not a crime, pedophiles are just ill. Therefore is there any wonder why pedophiles are attracted to this religion, ***"God says it's ok and the church will protect me.***" *This is sickening and the essence of pure evil.*

Priest Hole

This term was given to places made for hiding catholic priests that were allegedly persecuted by England in 1558. Seems an uprising in the north of England, by the Christians to depose the queen failed and at that time an act was passed against all Roman Catholics and the church, from engaging in their rites of faith. Those failing to take an Oath of Supremacy were called Recusants and were found guilty and could face death for high treason.

Seems one part of the god people (Christians), at this time, did not like the laws and plots to overthrow the non Roman Christian queen were afoot and they wanted to replace her with a Roman Catholic queen.   Like John F. Kennedy, he was just not Christian enough,,, and these people will have their way or they will kill you.

Global Financial Super Heating

Chapter Twelve

The High Ground

Global Financial Super Heating

Global Financial Super Heating

The term **High Ground** is a military expression and the goal of any army to achieve when in war. When one obtains the high ground, one can see ones enemy all around and can more easily destroy them.

I don't think they know it, but the atheists are standing on the high ground and don't seem to want to seize it. Most atheists I know of are just trying to show the world, '*see, I am a nice person too*' and I say, why do they have to prove they are nice? Atheists are not members of a cult and don't rape kids and cover it up. Or invade countries that have done nothing to us. They are clearly standing on the high ground and they need to wake up, seize it and seize it now! We all need to hear the truth.

This year ISIS has overrun Iraq and now use American weapons to kill off other Muslims that are not godly enough and to come after the terrorist invaders and occupiers of their land,,, Christian America. The people I talk to in this country (America) are sick of all the killing and now to lose the land we gained for the oil companies, makes most of us sick. But I understand why they want us off their land and out of their country,,, Americans are terrorist invaders, child murdering Christian led Nazis committing genocide. Yes, I said it - this Christian America is no different than Christian Nazi Germany.

The high ground, to some, is to refer to this Iraq war as the modern day **Christian Crusades**, for a Christian president invaded a country that did nothing to us so as to kill Muslims and take their land. It was about God for him, military armaments for others and of course oil and at the top,,, **The BIG 3**.

Now maybe that is a little strong for some of you and should be toned down, but you get the point. I personally think we should all tell the truth and tell it like it is and like we understand it to be. *(As I am doing, even if I am wrong on some points.) The* atheists should seize the **High Ground** and tell the truth to the American people. Most know they have been lied to, they just don't know what the lie is,,, so let the atheists tell them. *Who better?*

Christians and all other religions give atheists the tools they need, the **High Ground** all the time if only they would take it. In the litany of thou shalt not's found in the manual of teacher-minister, they show us all another of their **Achilles Heels**. Seems the good Christians just don't like **Bad Ink**.

The term **Bad Ink** is used to describe bad press or one of the dreaded thou shalt not's,,, **embarrassment**. And there it is,another Christian weak spot. The soft part of the underbelly of this beast is exposed and I use the words of the beast.

*"**Dishonesty** will not be tolerated,,, conviction of a **felony** and to cause public **embarrassment** or discredit. "*
From the manuals of teacher-minister

Those are the key words to bring down this great criminal enterprise and expose the powerful horned beast behind it,,, **dishonest, felony and embarrassment**. Their words,,, their rules,,, their game.

Fact - within the Christian ranking system **all** that have knowledge of a **felony** are **guilty** of **covering** it up. Now slow down and read this! The pope allegedly dismissed over 500 pedophiles from this church (that we know of) and to this day **conceals their names from prosecution**. And yet the pope, as leader of this religious cult and, (some think) **international criminal organization**, moves freely from country to country using an **alias name**. The people under him that have **knowledge of these crimes** and **aid and abet in the cover up, are all guilty of a felony** in America. And yet no one is arrested or prosecuted for one of the biggest cover ups of the past 100 years in America. Reminds you of the banksters because they are part of the same system of deceit and for the most part they (banksters that broke the law) are, or claimed to be, Christians and Jews. I know because I looked most of them up.

They may in fact have the power to conceal, cover up, or elude prosecution, but I believe, with truth on their side, the atheists can take the **High Ground** from them. Exposing their crimes as pedophiles and pursuing each one of them will become the atheists' Nuremburg trials. Endless pursuit by all atheists and exposure of all those that commit and cover up this most heinous of crimes,,, the raping of a child. That child is scarred for life and this church hides the guilty because (per the church) pedophilia is not a crime,,, it's an illness.

Dishonesty, Felony, Embarrassment

The Christians' Achilles Heel comes from their own words and actions. They use the word **Cult** to describe any other religion that is not theirs and disqualifies them from representing God. But the description of a **cult**, their words, (many think) describes themselves. Christianity is a cult by their own definition. The atheists need to take away their (the Christians) self appointed respect and their claim to the high ground by using their own words against them. Remember always **dishonesty, felony, embarrassment** and when they are on the run,,, keep pushing from all sides.

Global Financial Super Heating

The sheer magnitude of the pedophiles within the church and their cover up of this most heinous of crimes and should be exposed every chance atheists get. The following is a pyramid showing the potential of criminals within the church.

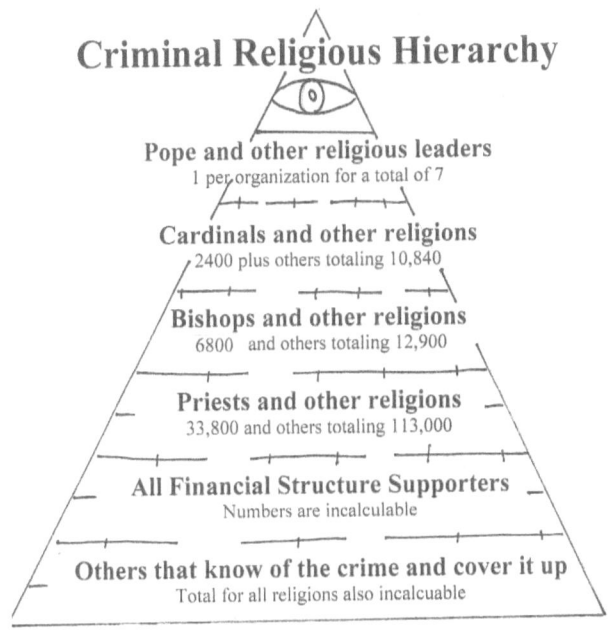

Criminal Religious Hierarchy

Pope and other religious leaders
1 per organization for a total of 7

Cardinals and other religions
2400 plus others totaling 10,840

Bishops and other religions
6800   and others totaling 12,900

Priests and other religions
33,800 and others totaling 113,000

All Financial Structure Supporters
Numbers are incalculable

Others that know of the crime and cover it up
Total for all religions also incalcuable

Estimated total number of criminals within this system covering up crimes against children and pedophiles are beyond this writer's imagination capabilities.

Sometimes when I see a cross around the neck of a follower of the Christian god, the conversation sometimes goes like this.

Pedophile Pitch

"Oh, I see you are a Christian."

"Yes, I am."

"Do you follow their teaching completely?"

"Yes indeed, Jesus is my savior."

"The pope is your leader and you follow his teachings and his word is next to God,,, right?"

"Yes."

"Do you think pedophiles are a bad thing?"

"Yes of course."

"The pope refuses to release the names of the pedophiles kicked out of the church. He is protecting them from prosecution and you're telling me you support that?"

"Aaaa."

"You think pedophiles are ok and if a priest wanted to have your son do a special job for God,,, that would be ok with you,,, is that right?"

"Aaaa, well no, of course not."

"But your pope stands next to God and he is committing a crime, a felony and you just said you support him."

"Well I,,,"

"And what about president Bush a Christian that invaded Iraq, a country that did nothing to America, so he could steal their oil and kill Muslims?"

Global Financial Super Heating

By now they are walking away tucking that cross into their shirt. The goal has been met by shoving **Dishonesty, Felony, and Embarrassment** in their face. I have used this on good Christians and it works. My final parting words, *"Well, whatever you do don't let your kids be alone with the priest or he will rape them."*

Christians are always selling their god to the masses and the church has a good sales team. So I suggest the atheists use such hard sales pitches as theirs (Christian) and the atheists can load the lips of all atheists with such pitches as the previous **Pedophile Pitch**.

Another pitch is whenever I do something nice for another person and a Christian tells me *"what you did was a good Christian act"* I jump back at them and say, *"Don't call me a Christian,,, I don't want to have sex with little boys!!!"* It generally puts them back in their shell and you don't have to listen to their Christian crap of murder and rape.

All religious people hate all atheists because they threaten their belief system. Just by being,,, they challenge them and their illness and that is where all the anger and hate comes from. If their religion and god were real, they would welcome the chance to save our souls. But as in a Spartanburg soup kitchen in South Carolina, reportedly atheists were turned away from helping the homeless.

Reportedly the leader of this soup kitchen a ███████████ said *"she would resign from her job* *before she would let atheists volunteer and be a <u>disservice</u> to this community. This is a ministry to serve God. We stand on the principles of God. Do they think our guests are so ignorant that they don't know what an atheist is?"*

I do so wonder what she thinks an atheist is. I wrote her a letter asking her to expand on her statements for this book and her response was *"no comment."* Too bad, I wanted to know just what such a good Christian thought an atheist was.

Once more Christians are calling out for help and showing us how desperate they are and in need of psychological treatment. It is so clear they are trying to give away the high ground and crying out for help. For me such a response of hate from a minister of God brings up two different responses when faced with such Christian evil.

1) A good response to her Christian hateful comments would be to say, "I can feel the love, or once more Christians are showing us all, their true love", the evil that is in their god.

2) Just what do atheists stand for? What have they been told behind those walls that divide us? Someone please tell me,,, what do Christians think atheists are. One told me with a shocked look on her face, "Well we are on opposite ends." *So I have my first clue,,, there are sides and we are not all people.*

I propose one of the platforms the atheists could stand for is exposing all religious criminals to the light of justice. But I can find no atheist platform or list of principles that they have. So I propose they build such a list of principles for all atheists to review and add suggestions as to what they do indeed stand for.

Keep it simple.

Pillars of Heaven

One of the most bazaar examples of the understanding of life is found in the Jewish concept of earth and heaven. Now remember Christianity has stolen Judaism's preaching,,, as they look up to an executed dead criminal bastard Jew man-god.

Jew heaven is an example of prehistoric man's attempts to understand man's place in and on the flat land called Earth. I found several examples of this Jew heaven and compiled all the drawing I could find, into one. If you ask a Jew today about all the silliness in their religion some will say, "it's just stories."

The following drawing is taken from several Jew Heaven examples I could find but do not show Second Heaven or Third Heaven. Is this the place where Christians will be serving the Jews and their Jew god?

Jew Heavens

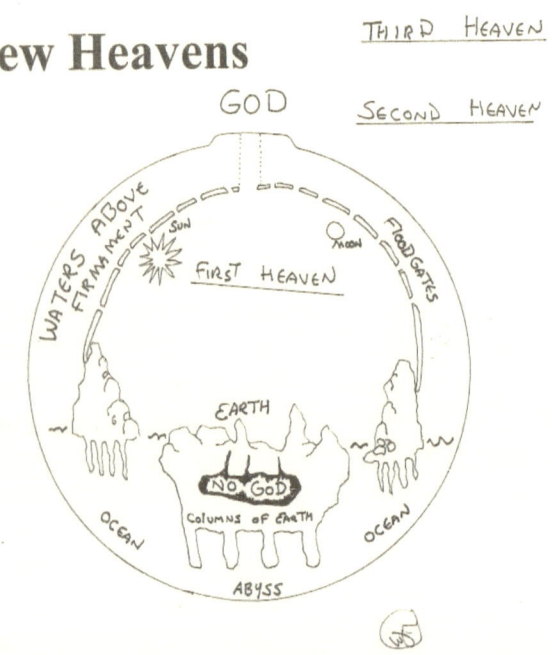

We get this from selected men (only)
that pray to a wall.

That may help explain it.

Oh yeah, this is what the place that I want to avoid when I die looks like.

Followers of Judaism, Jehovah and Islam are not free of this pedophile cover up and should also be hunted down like the dogs they are. No wait, that is wrong, dogs are better than them and I like most dogs because they are mostly truthful and honest,,, unlike people of God.

Summarizing to this point

It is most difficult to predict the future for none of us have a crystal ball and the following is my attempt to look forward in time. I hope I am wrong but believe if we do nothing, this is going to happen and we all need to prepare. However you chose to move forward in time is your choice and the worst that would happen is you would be prepared,,, however you believe is best.

1. Financial disaster is just on the horizon if certain events transpire, as I predict that based on history and events that are unfolding before our eyes, they will. The crash of the global **god/notes.**
2. Super heating will be a result of our reckless consumption and God given right to own one of everything. The crash of the **god/notes** will cause economic disaster for the airlines as the sky becomes bluer and burns off the water we drink and kills the food we eat.

3. Wars over food and water with rampant disease will cross the globe killing many people. Starvation and death will become commonplace as no one will be isolated from what is to come. If you have food and water,,, they will come to take it from you.

4. As countries fall, because of their failing dollar or extreme weather, the military will take over and **martial law** will be the rule of the land. Political prisoners will be housed in concentration work camps with other unwanted people - like the handicapped and mentally ill.

5. Because of the crash of the global **god/note,** across the world, people will not work for free and must walk away from their jobs for lack of pay or what they are paid will not pay the bills and feed the family. Therefore power plants will not have the money to or willingness to spend the money needed to maintain the decaying plants and radioactive waste will just drain onto the land, into the air and sea as they (the 1%-ers) just walk away pockets filled with green paper.

6. Within this country, the United States of America, this government has plans for its people that I did not see coming and I believe it is for that time,,, when the truth comes out. I only became aware of this mind numbing information in October of this year and I have expanded on it in

Chapter Thirteen. It is a future I did not see coming - **if** the information I have found is true. However, it does make logical sense if you look at life as the **BIG 3** would.

Atheist in the Future

I believe this is the time for people of "**the none of the above" category** need to stand up and organize ourselves and their power. As they stand now they are splinter groups at best, but if they can find a way to all get on the same page,,, you are talking about one fifth of the world population at this time.

The following are examples of moving forward that I make as suggestions only. I am not looking to lead an organization and to face off the religious wackos of the world. There are things we, as individuals, can do that will send a strong message to the religions of the world. Ghandi was but one peaceful man that helped change the world and fight off the Christian invaders, without firing a shot or killing one person. However he did end up dead, executed on January 30, 1948 for what I understand to be God, money and land. *Christian values.*

1. There is one political party in America (the rich) split into two parts. The far right

appears to be made up of all Christians and they are mostly Republicans and then there are the Democrats on the left. The far right stands for all things good and Christian and now Democrats, like left handed people are evil and a sign of the devil. But now, for the most part, do and say the same things as Republicans and follow the same god. *The frightening part is when one of the Christian wacko leaders invites both of the candidates, Republican and Democrat, to speak before their Christian church in a sort of Christian debate he states he is not telling his followers who to vote for, but holds up both as approved by the Christian church.* Changing your affiliation to independent sends a message to both sides of this **one party.**

2. Taking the High Ground with the truth on their side should be the atheists' top priority, by exposing all religious criminal pedophiles to justice. Hunting each one down and exposing them and their crimes to the police for their arrest should become our top concern. Not just the one that did the crime but all that knew of the crime and helped cover it up. I am speaking of and suggesting only the arrest of the pope for his crimes against these children and all Americans as their single and top priory.

3. Organizing all atheists under one central form of leadership, however is best, would put a face to intelligence and truth. I am personally drawn to the American Indians' concept of leadership. There can be several War Chiefs until one is chosen as the chief, or leader, of all atheists. There could be several Chiefs; I like an odd number to always break a tie.

4. Examples like Salton Lake were provided in this book to show forward thinking for all of us in the tribe to survive and do no harm to the planet. They should incorporate the word atheist in each example and as in this one, change the name from Salton Lake to Atheist Lake or Lake Atheist where all are welcomed. Gays, women and other Christian throw-away-people would be welcomed at Lake Atheist. Even people suffering from **scrupulosity** (provided they are getting help from proper licensed psychological professionals) would be welcomed. This will send ripples across the globe within the religious community and provide all atheists with the Good Ink and a platform to speak - not pillars to stand on above everyone else. From such a point atheists would always ask for help to hunt down the Christians within their church, (as well as other religions) that know of the

crimes committed by the pedophiles and the ones that helped cover it up.

5. Labels,,, are very powerful and atheists can use them as stepping stones to gain more and more of that high ground. Examples are, 'all Christians are pedophiles, if you support Christ you support pedophiles' and so on. The point is to push the crimes Christians are committing and draw them out. If truly good Christian people come forward and tell their story of rape, and concealment of the same, to the police, others will follow and down it will start to come. The pope may think pedophiles are suffering from a sickness or they are just ill,,, but the goal is to have him do that from an American jail cell.

Looking forward

New record temperatures are coming across the globe every year now, no matter what we do, via burning of fossil fuels giving us carbon dioxide to breath. High gear heating of the planet will hit with the next major global financial depression. No matter who causes it, all will crash because all countries to my knowledge have adapted the **god/note**, theirs or ours. If it happens a week from now, ten years or 50 years, it is going to happen.

Global Financial Super Heating

Food will become scarce and more expensive. Only the rich will eat as we all become farmers or thieves stealing food to feed our families. This September, 2014, a major meat producer in America was sold to China so they can feed their growing middle class. We get the hog shit and they get our food. Reportedly at the same time it was said that one quarter of all grain produced in this country goes to China. And the tipping point is just starting.

Good clean drinking water will become scarce in many parts of the world and people will migrate. Even public works like Oregon with its E-coli outbreak this year, 2014, warning close to 700,000 people to boil their drinking water, will become more common place. And then there is all that **Hydraulic Fracking** to make money for the oil companies, under the pretext of filling a need. When all we need to do is have the Christian federal government stop using the 50% of all the oil used in America pushing one god over another. Just come home.

A platform of honesty and truth is needed across the globe and I suggest that atheists build such upon the high ground it will seize. A platform one step out of the mental mud of life - not set on pillars above all the other people where atheists can preach down to them. A ranking system for all atheists that wish to participate be created as all religions and religious governments are attacked for their crimes against people,,, all life and the Earth. This is an ongoing relentless attack of the god people across the globe.

The following is a suggestion only, for an **Atheist Ranking System** for I can fine none. This is not meant as a recruitment drive of atheists but is my attempt to help all people find the truth. We all know there is little truth in religion, so why not turn to people that do not suffer from the mental illness, scrupulosity? If that would help organize all atheists everywhere around the world, then maybe the rest of the world can get to some of the truth, concealed by the **BIG 3**.

No longer would they be splinter groups or social clubs that meet for coffee and tea, but would become soldiers in a war to stop all religions from destroying the planet in God's name. We all must stand up to stop the killing of innocent people and our children's futures, by these god people willing to destroy the planet and all that is on it for their god and only their god is the right god.

Atheist Ranking System
Suggestions only

Atheists: any persons - gays, women, men that understand there is no god. Religion is only for a small, weak, and needy mind trying to understand a complicated world.

Militant Atheist Soldier: one willing to stand up and be counted as against all religions and all gods and add his/her voice to the cause.

Atheist Warrior: one willing to face off the evil that is religion,,, with intelligent peaceful acts that may be interpreted as disobedient and put them at risk of losing their freedom, liberties and well being for the cause of exposing the crimes of the god people. Example; even though you have a permit to protest outside a church that committed a crime against a child you could be arrested for some trumped up crime.

Atheist Warrior Chief: selected to this ranking by vote from a region or an area because of their leadership in the cause of all atheists. Causes being, to dismantle all religions that kill, rape, invade and bring harm to people and the planet, by exposing their crimes through peaceful means. They must attack religions, for this is where the evil is, not God. Let the sick and weak have this God-crutch,,, for they need it. Example: Amish are peaceful, non- warring Christians that don't want to kill every one that is non Christian and take their land.

Supreme Chief: would be one of highest ranking spokespersons. There would be several, recommending guidance to all soldiers in the battle against religious ignorance, superiority and intolerance of others. Not unlike the UN, where one from each country/state/county could speak and provide suggestions for management of the planet in the future.

Elder Militant Atheist: highly respected person to aid in the guidance of the meek that will inherit the earth after the god people are gone. We don't want another Jamestown Kool-Aid incident brought on by these people that suffer from a psychological disorder,,, **Scrupulosity**. No one wants them dead, (unlike the god people) just clean up the mess they have made in God's name.

The goal of all **Militant Atheist Soldiers** should be to expose the criminal element within all religions from a platform (not a pedestal) of truth and not from ignorance and hate as the religions do. Remembering at all times that their (the religions) Achilles heel is **Dishonesty, Felony and Embarrassment.** This is the Achilles heel of Christianity and I am willing to bet all other **cult** religions have the same. It is time to send these god people (all religions) back to their **Priest Hole** where they belong,,, in the history of the dark ages.

The single endless goal of all atheists should be to track down every criminal within all religions that has committed a felony against a child (especially by a pedophile), including those that aid in the cover-up of that crime. Forming coalitions with law enforcement and the media, to force their hand to expose these crimes and prosecute. If the police and courts don't prosecute,,, move up the ladder and force the issue.

Global Financial Super Heating

It may be up to atheists to start to clean up the world (if that can be done) as we move forward in time by exposing ignorance to the light of intelligence. One thing clear about this life, we all just want to enjoy it for what it is. Like a playground, the one thing we are all discovering is tourism is good for us all. The whole planet benefits from tourism and that one fact should help explain the greater call of us all. It's not God, heaven, the afterlife or the almighty **god/notes**, but the stewardship of this thin blue space we all share and all want to enjoy. This is a thread that runs through us all,,, we just want to have fun, experience and enjoy life. From a time when we were small and could first understand life, we just wanted to play and have fun with others. Puppies play with cats, birds play with squirrels and so on. Life is to be enjoyed and not endured. This is not a test of God, for if it were, all god people would fail. For religion does not bring people together to do good, but it separates people so they can do harm, for they are superior to the rest of us, behind their walls and against those that are not part of their cult.

The demographics for the atheists are small and reportedly only comprise about two percent of the planet's population so, by those numbers, atheists have an uphill battle. The number jumps up to about eighteen percent when you add in the non-religious of the world or the agnostics. But there are three more comrades in the war (on ignorance, bias, hatred, intolerance and separation) that we all are fighting:

1.) The Christian church has kicked out all gay and lesbian people (as well as all blacks that we don't talk about); atheists should welcome them and their fight and right to be part of life.

2.) Black people or dark skinned people will never be part of the hierarchy of the Christian religion and will never be more than slaves and property to these holy god people. People of color can never rise above their race in the system of **Casta** (Christian system of Spanish separation of black/African ancestry) unless their brown skin is bred out of them in four generations, as I understand. This system excludes all black people for their color cannot be bred out of them per the Spanish church of the 1700s. Casta is a Spanish word used to describe people from the Philippines in a system to categories of mixed race people. They (black and people of color) are like we goyim in the Jewish religion, except goyim does include white people.

3.) All women are just property to these men of God as they try to control every aspect of their lives by ostracizing and controlling them. Time to welcome them to a better life and tell them to take off their Hijab and come out of the dark ages to the light of intelligence found within the 21st century. All women should be welcomed as equals.

A suggestion would be to have the exposure of **Dishonesty, Felony and Embarrassment** become one of the first planks that atheists build their platform on the high ground. The fourth plank (no particular order) of atheism should be **stewardship**. It's time for all mankind to lift our snouts out of the mental muck and mud of life and wake up to the evil that is religion and take action for all living things,,, to try to save what is left from the evil that is in all religions.

At the outset of this book I had no idea how depressing the future looked and how close we all are to the end of life as we know it. I blamed all Christians at first, for their acts of evil and hatred for others unlike them, but they are not alone and if it were not them, it would be another cult herding us all into pens to be controlled (Judaism, Muslim to name but a few). But I have come to understand they are taught to be sick and can't help it. All religious people seem to suffer from **Scrupulosity,** a psychological disorder whereby the sufferer of this disorder believes or has been convinced they are going to hell. Some suffering from this disorder believe they must confess to every sin (as reportedly did Martin Luther King) or they will burn in hell. Afraid to live and afraid to die,,, they are sick and need help.

Mass Psychogenic Illness or Mass Hysteria or collective hysteria or group hysteria are all part of collective obsession behavior disorder, if I understand it correctly. It starts to sound like all people within all religions. We all seem to yearn to belong to something and be part of a greater,,, something,,, but how about something that does good, real good and welcomes all types and all colors of people,,, like atheism.

Another plank for the atheist platform, to try to do no harm and only do good,,, unlike people of religion.

To me it is a sign of insanity to do the same thing over and over and expect a different outcome. I therefore have changed the placement of my blame for all the world's ills from all religions to all atheists. For it is those that understand, like atheists, that have quietly stood by and let these nut jobs take over and kill everything in the name of their gods.

Recapping the book to this point

1. **God/notes** are crashing, tangibles like gold and silver are not.
2. Global Shading is real and is going to change life on earth for a very long time.
3. Carbon dioxide levels are going to peak off the charts and are, as we speak, moving straight up higher than they have ever been in the known recorded history of earth. This man-made outcome will be with us for a

long,,, long,,, long,,, time, if we are here to see it.

4. Water and food will disappear sooner rather than later.

5. Atheism can grow if the atheists unite as defenders of children and the planet, pointing out all the destructive actions of the god people.

There is no doubt the future is bleak at best and unless we earthlings do something to stop the spike of carbon dioxide,,, there will be **no** earth,,, **no** life. The point I would like each of us to walk away with is, as long as we each do nothing,,, nothing will change. The near future is full of changes and if we prepare, we earthlings as a species, may survive. Waiting until the end or when change is forced upon you, is too late. There is little time left to do the right thing and I do not want to leave this planet looking back and say, "That's just too bad,,, gods destroyed it all and I did nothing to stop it."

I want to emphasize one last point about man's ignorance of his delicate environment and the destructive actions we earthlings take without understanding the ramifications and consequences. One small thing can affect the world and all life in a very devastating manner - like global warming; this is another item swept under the carpet of life, to protect us all from the truth.

Fish tank Stem Plants

After covering all the destructive points I have in this book, why would I bring up such an innocent subject? After all who among us does not like to see something small and free, imprisoned for our joy and pleasure? It's only when we grow tired of all the daily feedings and other care we must give these small creatures that depend on us, that the trouble begins.

The fish die or we move and can't take them with us and we don't want to kill them so we set them free by dumping them in lakes, streams or the ocean. The fish may or may not live for a short time but the plants,,, live on forever.

I can find little information on the Christian/American government edited internet, other than how to buy these plants. Reportedly these plants,,, specifically the Hornwort or Ceratophyllum Echinatum or Anthocerotopsida is such a stem plant that grows like a weed and covers everything in its path.

As I understand this plant started out as something growing off the coast of Australia and one type was harvested and used to make fish tanks look nicer, with a spot of green. It was so successful that this weed crossed the globe in just a matter of decades and now, as I understand, is everywhere on the planet.

So why should I care? This is a very healthy, vibrant plant that has virtually no enemies for the most part. Tests have proven that ice and darkness will kill the plant. People are dumping this stem plant into the sea across the globe and now it is taking root,,, everywhere.

Reportedly this plant now is found in the Mediterranean Sea (as an example) and is growing at an alarming rate. It is covering the sea floor and killing all other sea life. Coral reefs, once full of fish and crabs, are now smothered with this fast growing plant, that nothing can eat and nothing can kill.

If the small fish have no place to live and nothing to eat what will the bigger fish eat? And down the line it travels until we get back to man. It was also reported this plant was found in a bay in California clogging boats propellers and upsetting the rich. Now it's a problem.

I am not making this up... the rich tried everything until they discovered some highly toxic poison that killed everything. I think it was copper sulfate that is known to kill bacteria, algae, roots, plants, snails, fungi and plants. Now the rich can happily motor around the dead bay.

Gene hacking and Bio hacking

There is a new industry growing in the world and so many see this as the computer industry of the 70s and 80s. **I am not making this up**. People across the globe are engaging in do-it-yourself body enhancements and **in home gene sequencing**. These want-a-be billionaires are gene splicing plants to grow all manner of unregulated new species like trees that glow in the dark. What will happen when one of these unregulated nut jobs mixes the Hornwort stem plant with let's say,,, lawn grass? Nothing can kill it, it will always be nice and green and when you trim your Hornwort Grass,,, every bit of chopped up plant will grow a new plant. Because it is fast growing, some estimates of the Hornwort are up to four inches per day, it could cover the globe in just a few years.

The options are limitless. What if they grow a new fungus that can't be killed, that loves to live in human lungs? How do you stop that?

My fear is whatever we do to educate people just will not be enough and it is too late to stop what is to come. This is but another very dark and scary road we earthlings are going down all for the accumulation of as many **god/notes** in our short life we can get and the king status all people seem to seek.

As we age our views change and the desire of ownership of one of everything subsides. It's a lot of work to be king and some discover less is better.

The following is a comical and satirical look forward in time as to what I believe will be coming up in this century. You may find that the following detracts from the devastation I see coming but I cannot help who I am and how the creative part of my mind works. I have been told the 21st Century Business, God or Satan, What would they say? and Planting Flowers do not belong in this book. But they poured out of my mind in flashes of creativeness as I was writing this book. If not here, where else?

21st Century Business

As I try to look forward into the upcoming new/old dark ages that all antiquated, goat herding religions have brought upon the land that we all share, I try to see the best place to position myself and my investing dollars. If I had kids I would want to have them trained in these future businesses.

Because the evil and ignorance that is religion will turn us backwards in time, to its days of greatness, this will bring about investment opportunities that we can get in on the ground floor. One need only look at the past to see the future and there is much gold lying on the ground just waiting for smart people to pick up.

Some of the following are meant as humorous, but I fear, knowing people as I do,,, that these are very real.

Slavery: is a fast growing business across the globe these days and a smart investor will get in on this one quickly. Of course your clients will protect you and you should seek out good customers like Christian congressmen and senators. They will ensure there will be **no investigation** (as there is none now). But the best customers would be church leaders, for they have grown tired of all the bad ink in the past few years and the P.O.P.E. does not want to pay to cover this up any more. So each church owning their own child sex slaves is the best investment for them. Even if you would have to give the first few away (sell them cheap) to prime the pump. I am looking to invest my dollars in a startup company called, **Abstinence Incorporated**. Motto; *"let us bring the fun back into sex with children, without scrutiny."*

Slavery Accompaniments: will be another good investment for our dollars of the future, as this new industry will have a need for leg irons,,, in a variety of sizes.

    Small, for those little feet that may want to run home to mommy or worse,,, away from God and their new owners and all that fun *"God has a* *job for you little boy":* sex. The church motto is *"get them by eight or it's too late."*

  Medium, for all the young women sold into prostitution, also more interested in freedom rather than their jobs, providing sex and new children born into slavery that can bring a good return on our invested dollars.

  Large, for when that child grows into a man and our customers grow tired of them and he or she can be sold to a religious government work camp, working for god.

  Of course we will need lots of **Whipping Posts**, **Iron Collars** that bolt to the walls and **Auction Blocks** to show off the product being sold. And for the good Christians - they will require **Impaling Poles**, life size **Crosses** and my favorite, **The Hinged Wheel**, for the allotment of punishment and display for all to see. *Yes, good times are a comin',,, praise the lord.*

Entertainment: traveling shows that tour the country with performances like the Roman days in the coliseum. The unwanted, undesirable and unbelievers of all religions would be brought to the show and fed to the lions, used as archery practice and chopped up for fun and profit for all to see and enjoy. *A great place to bring the family and see what happens when one falls out of favor and likeness with god.*

Drugs: will be with us for all time and as we pass over this little <u>war on drugs thing</u>, (as opposed to doctor care with clean prescribed drugs and treatment to get people off drugs) this business will finish growing and come to its full potential. Children will be taught in the classroom how to shoot up and tell good drugs from the inferior type. Don't worry about the police, the jails will be full and there will not be money to incarcerate them all. Plus K Street will pave the way with gold for the good Christian congressmen and senators (those poli-Christian) and new laws will finally protect the poor little drug dealer, as they now protect the large pharmaceutical drug dealers and the doctor drug dealers that kill people (without prosecution).

I offer an example of one small pharmacy here in the Tampa bay area that sold a record amount (and by record I mean more than sold annually in some states,,, sold in this one store) of addictive pharmaceutical drugs in one year. This pharmacy sold 750 pills to a girl, with a prescription from a doctor and she died of an overdose. The tragedy here, besides the murder of a child, is that the pharmaceutical company knew this one store was a drug dealing pharmacy and did not alert authorities. But they did cash all the checks. To the best of my knowledge no one went to jail for her murder (not the doctor, not the pharmacy, and not the manufacturer).

Then all these fine and legal drug companies (not to be confused with the other fine and legal, addictive drug manufactures) will enter the stock market and be gobbled up like pharmaceutical drugs stolen from your grandfather. I will be looking for the name, **Christian Drug Cartel Incorporated**, motto, *"our pathway to bring you closer to God with chemicals."*

Water Filtration: will be a hot product as long as it removes that pesky radiation now found to be draining from the poorly stored power plants; as well as hydraulic fracturing chemicals (that are unknown by federal law) and soon coming to a home near you; toxins, bio-hazards, old oil and other unwanted products from manufacturers that it is just cheaper to dump on the highway rather than pay to properly dispose; and, finally, removing that natural gas coming from our drinking water that you can set on fire and that boiling can't seem to remove.

Air Filtration: for the home, office and your car will also be a good product as long as it removes radiation, evaporated hydraulic fracturing chemicals, gas, and other man-made toxins coming from the earth into the air and into our homes. *Motto; take your last breath from us.*

Wearable Coolers: these are devices that permit all the good Christian people (as opposed to slaves) to go outside during the day, without the discomfort from the new summer heat. Additional marketing benefits would be that each slave could be permanently fitted with this garment so they can work the fields longer while testing the water and environment for their Christian masters. I can envision all people left on the earth must wear such garments to enter the hostile moonscape that is to become earth.

War mongering: is an old business like prostitution, slavery, voodoo and God, but will do well in the next 100 years as the clock is turned back. The future need for new tools such as an electronic witch and warlock detector built on the premise of a type of electric feedback monitor the lost in space people use. The monitor's controller interpretations will decide the fate of the one charged under the new martial law,,, as the Nazis did when sending people to work or the showers.

Dungeons and torture chambers: will become a big local business like health clubs. The need to find and extract the truth (Christian truth) from accused witches, warlocks, unwanted wives, and other nonbelievers will be necessary. As all atheists will have to go underground to survive, like the abortion doctors, Jews, women, blacks, gays and atheists will be against the law. As for me I plan to open one of these *"God will help find the truth"* stores. I know there must be Christians out there that have not confessed to **all their sins** and I will help them. Oh yes,,, with much joy I will extract those Christian confessions,,, so God may have these people in the next life and the rest of us will know where they all are,,, so we can avoid them.

Incarceration: also will become a very big

business only it must be done on a grander scale and cheaply. First we have to get rid of all these pesky and costly laws that protect people's rights. Then to lower the cost even more let's get rid of all those unsightly prisons and put them all in one place. Such a good and viable location may be found in my book *The Copper Pit*.

Education and brain washing: of

the next generation will be a top priority of the Christian mafia. Prayer in school will be first then in the work place. Anyone failing to comply will be sent to the **God Loves You Work Camps**, for additional training and electric shock therapy. If that fails, the severing of limbs will become necessary to convince the ungodly that god is real and loves you. And from the schools, the chosen ones, (pretty young blond children) will be given a very special task to serve God in a special way. The motto will be *baptize them when born and have slaves for life.*

Healthy DNA: will be a growing business as the experimentation of the 20th century and first part of the 21st century is exposed. Allegedly, all of this experimentation on our DNA with those pills the pharmaceutical companies created and all those vaccination shots given to kids will have taken their devastating toll.

Generations of defective kids will have been born and repairing these new pharmaceutical defects will be a priority. The big prize will go to the one that finds the defect in the genes that creates atheists, Jews, Muslims, agnostics, blacks and gays. Finally, a cure for these twisted thinkers that don't fall in line and march to the Christian drummer boy, will be permanently gone and the earth will see a new super race of Christians. We can call this jean the Christian Master Race Gene. *Motto; Gott mit uns, (God with us) finally the right and only god.*

Hired guns: are not new and as the Christian total colonization continues, the need to finally kill off the competition will be necessary,,, and fun too. Like Uganda, I can see one day the good Christians in America will create a **Kill All the Gays Law** as well and when you find them,,, just kill them.

The ***thou shalt not kill*** thing won't apply to them because as far as Christians are concerned, gays are not people, they are some type of goyim. This dehumanizing will continue and soon after Jews, Muslims and atheists will be annexed into this new law. *There are just too many people anyway, so why should we share this space with the bad and defective ones?*

Pulling teeth: will be another big business in the next 100 years as people become poorer, no one will have money to see a dentist,,, like today,,, so it will be up to back room masters of pliers to remove the unwanted pain. You can spot the poor by their smiles.

Coat hanger abortions: are going to come out of the past in a big way (as the Christians push their religion on the rest of us) and become another home remedy to the problem of another mouth to feed.

Seems Christians force us to keep unwanted babies, but don't offer to pay for them. My thinking is if the church forces these children on the rest of us then they should pay for them,,, school and prison.

Only bad part for the Christians is they would have to part with some of that gold they have and that god of theirs just will not have that. It took so long to get and to give it up to feed babies,,, no way. Let them eat grass.

Global Financial Super Heating

Chapter Thirteen

Martial Law and Death Camps

Fact or Fiction?

Paranoia?

American tax dollars pay to kill Palestinian people.

Can This Be True?

In October of this year 2014, I was informed of much of the following information discovered quite by accident by a friend. I knew when I saw this that it was to go into this book at this point. My chin hit the top of my desk and I still find it hard to believe that no one else that I know knows of this or is talking about this (if it is true).

Now it should be known that I try to watch the broadcast news every day (what is permitted to filter down to the poor). I watch the Germen news, I watch the Asian news, I watch the English news and I watch the American news,,, plus I watch broadcast news magazine programs and up to this point felt I was well informed as to current events.

What I saw from my friend, mixed so well with what I knew, that many of the remaining pieces fell into place in a startling and frightening manner. Just when I think I know and just when I think I understand, new pieces of the puzzle of life come in to fill the empty spaces, creating the bigger, clearer picture. I would like to think I am wrong and this is not true, but all arrows point to this one system neatly laid out before me,,, **The BIG 3**.

Ten Regions
within the USA
and the
Superior Body

Now keep in mind **The BIG 3** and who is at the top pulling the strings,,, The String Master. This self appointed **Deity** slowly taking over the world,,, or he or they already own it and are just laying out the steps to claim their prize,,, **total control over us all.**

They cannot claim this prize if we are informed and educated and know how to step around their power points over us. Edward Snowden is one such man that stepped out of line showing us pieces of the puzzle (that they in power, vehemently deny) that we did not see before. Thanks to him and people like Julian Assange founder of Wikileaks,,, that gave up everything for us,,, we have more information. It should be noted that these brave people risked their freedom and their lives bringing us this information and did not do it for money, like those in power that are trying to cover it up.

Global Financial Super Heating

Today Julian Assange is a wanted man for his part in releasing this information. Meanwhile news papers now have set up avenues for whistleblowers like Edward Snowden, and they (the papers releasing the information) are free. Or they, under orders from the **Deity** (owners of the papers), have established themselves as some type of Wikileaks. My question is: will they turn your information and you,,, over to this Christian government, never reporting your attempts to expose these national crimes and international crimes? You just go away.

Under the guidance of **The BIG 3,** the past **Deities** have tried to open up the world to one order since it was discovered that it was not flat. Japan, reportedly was opened up by Matthew Calbraith Perry in 1854 under the **American Open Door Policy**. Reportedly this was later replaced with the **Open Door Note** and then came the **Spheres of Influence** and then the **Soft Power**. I believe this was replaced later with the **League of Nations** established on January 10, 1920 after WWI, The **United Nations** was established to promote international co-operation on October 24, 1945, just after WWII and the world was divided up and new maps were drawn. It is my understanding, **ISIS** to this day is fighting these new maps and the Christians that have invaded their land,,, killing their people. This is their (Christian) track record and much like what they did in the Americas and are doing via Jews,,, in what is left of Palestine.

Global Financial Super Heating

Dehumanize the indigenous people, declare them as savages or terrorists and then kill them and take their land. *It's the American way.*

Allegedly, the United Nations passed a resolution that the United States **must** reorganize into 10 super regions. *Now stop and think for a moment,,, why would they care? Unless someone else like the Deity of the BIG 3 cared. It should be noted that the United States was divided up before by the banking system in The Federal Reserve Act of 1913. Banks, money, power, why not the military?* I can find no date or other information of this resolution from the U.N., however,,, President Richard Millhouse Nixon,,, did on February 14, 1972, sign executive order 11647 that created a **new** country now in 10 parts. Nixon (a Republican,,, Quaker,,, Christian) left office in disgrace after Watergate and did not go to jail for his crimes.

But his legacy will be the establishment of the new world order over us Americans, as he did with the signing of his name, replacing this government so many died for, believing in its values of free speech and separation of church and state. The **Deity** within **The BIG 3** has spoken, and the paid and enriched underlings step into place.

In my lifetime I have never heard one Senator or Congressmen speak out on this Executive Order #11647 that may (some believe will) take all power away from every level of this American elected government, from the Federal level to your home town leaders. Such power over us, the people, would never have passed our elected officials and the scrutiny of us Americans and yet this law is there,,, on the books,,, without so much as a whimper from us.

Build it and it will come

One cannot plan to take away the freedoms of us Americans under the pretenses of crises without the **planned** knowledge of these crises coming true or man-made crises such as nuclear, financial, riots and the scariest of them all,,, the Christians boogieman or the antichrist is to appear with visible angels. *When will this stupidity end?*

What type of freely (selected by the Deity) elected dictator would take over control of this country? We have seen such things in the past (and it is so close now) where the military once in power never let go. Of course they will tell us, "this is for your own good and you should be happy",,, or else!!!

Anything they do is ok if they keep away the boogieman.

Arbeit macht frei
work makes (you) free

The American people are just waking up to the reality that the federal government of the United States, founded on God Christian beliefs, reportedly has and is running concentrations camps within its borders,,, for its people. I am surprised to find this out, because I thought all people knew this was a fact. In WWI, **paranoia** raced through the veins of this government and the president at that time Woodrow Wilson under Executive Order, did proclaim that all *"persons of enemy birth"* must register with the government and if deemed a threat to this government could be incarcerated,,, without a trial. *See Civil Forfeiture in the United States.*

A threat to the government at this time would include, but not be limited to same, be as follows:

1. An **alien enemy** shall not write, print, or publish any attack on or threat against the government or congress.
2. An **alien enemy** shall not have any firearms.
3. An **alien enemy** shall not have or operate any aircraft.
4. An **alien enemy** shall not have or operate a wireless apparatus or any signaling device.

Global Financial Super Heating

The list goes on but you get the point. The president of the United States shall have reasonable cause to believe the **person of enemy of birth** is a danger and should be placed in **one of two camps** at that time. Camp one was in Fort Douglas, Utah and camp two was in Fort Oglethorpe, Georgia. Now this was April 1917.

All property of an **alien enemy** in violation shall be seized by the government. Why are these things surprising? Try getting on a plane today with $10,000.00 of your cash and see what happens. The police can take your car and sell it and keep the money and all your cash and you have not been found guilty of a crime. *This is the face of Marshal Law where you are guilty until proven innocent.* Actions of a police state you say? You may be right,,, but they are only taking things from the bad people,,, right? Subjective you say, be careful whom you say that to,,, for you could be next.

In WWII **"persons of enemy of birth"** were gathered up, under executive order 9066 signed by Franklin D. Roosevelt on February 19, 1942. Then by the tens of thousands,,, good American citizens of this country were herded into trains with their meager belonging and sent to American concentration camps. Some of these people were 3rd, 4th and 5th generation American citizens. *But this could never happen to you,,, so don't worry.*

Not only was it Japanese Americans but German and Italian American citizens went to the American concentration camps also, losing all their property, seized by this government, without due process of law. They just made it up (law) as they went along.

Over time we have gotten used to the federal government stepping in to help in times of disaster (like war). The face of that assistance has now become F.E.M.A. or the Federal Emergency Management Agency founded on June 19, 1978, as part of the Presidential Reorganization Plan No. 3 in 1970. This now is under the watchful eye of Homeland Security (the ones keeping all our phone records and internet history for us,,, and on us).

In April of 1925 a small, harmless Christian man had a need for some bodyguards and created a group with the best of intentions. Over time this good holy Christian man grew in power and his need for protection (or **paranoia**) also grew as his takeover of all power was being implemented. Guided by his faith and moving forward,,, led by God's hand,,, he created the **SS** to protect him and we all know or should know how that turned out. *Absolute power corrupts absolutely.*

If you look closely this **ten region system** of non-elected officials in America clearly takes on a military stance,,, as they (government laws and orders) all do when you look closely. Whatever is to happen is well within the plans for our near future as more and more government money is spent **secretly** to spy on us all.

Public Law 87-297, Arms Control and Disarmament act of 1961, signed into law on

Global Financial Super Heating

September 26, 1961, was I believe to be designed for apocalyptic armaments, weapons of mass destructions like nuclear. However the term **armaments,** is used within the law and this word can be used to describe objects like clubs, swords, sticks, and stones and oh yes,,, **guns**. *It must be for our own good,,, or maybe theirs. If they (the government) take our guns,,, only they and the crooks will have guns. We will be at their mercy,,, both sides,,, if there is a division from them (government/crooks).*

Are we all to become like Christian England? Will this Christian American government implement this law (87-297) and then come into your home and take away your dinner knifes as well as your guns to defend your home? They can't control you if you are educated and some believe,,, have a gun. Some people I know have told me, *"I will take out as many as I can when they come for me and my guns."* And another said, *"When they come for my guns they will get the bullets first."*

The foundation is there and now is up to interpretation by the descendants of its creators (like the bible and the Quran). All stepping into line under orders from,,, **not American elected leaders,,,** but as I have seen it called,,, **The Superior Body**. Each time we Americans go to war,,, we Americans must report to this Superior Body,,, for its authorization. We are not free.

There seems to be little point to go to Congress and ask them,,, for what is the need? The decision to go to war is not theirs (Congress) but falls into the laps of people not in or from this country,,, not Americans. We the American people of this country and all other countries on this globe allegedly report to and under one power,,, **The Superior Body** or sometimes known as the United Nations.

Now let's factor in **The BIG 3** and put yourself into their power position. Things (for the **BIG 3**) have been set up with the best of intentions and you want to take over the world. For me I always envision the **Deity** of **The BIG 3** as a little man wringing his hands together like Simon Bar Legree from the cartoons I loved to watch as a kid. But Simon always got caught in the end and went to jail. These people of the **BIG 3** hide well and strongly protect their own and you can see this everywhere today if you take the time to look.

If Simon the **Deity** of **The BIG 3** wanted to take over the world and control all money and all power what better place than to control The **Superior Body**. **Dark money** must flow like water in the United Nations for who is to watch it? What watch dog committee looks over world interests and the bribes that must take place here? If you wanted to control the world,,, what better place than here within the halls of the United Nations.

Law H. R. 645

Death Camps?

January 22, 2009
The establishment of national emergency centers.

To provide temporary housing, medical, and humanitarian assistance,,,

*Now isn't that nice? The leaders of America provided the same thing for the Germans in WWI and the Japanese, Italians and the Germans in WWII and now,,, who is to go into these camps during the never ending **War on Drugs and the War on Terrorism?***

To provide centralized locations to improve coordination of preparedness and not-for-profit entities and **faith-based organizations,,,**

*I thought the National Guard of each state did that but now we have protection for all the good religious people and their organizations,,, and there is that **Separation of Church and State** thing all over again. Is it the god people that will be coming for our guns and then the last of our freedoms?*

To meet other <u>appropriate needs</u>, as determined by the **Secretary of Homeland Security.**

*Would that open-ended term, '**appropriate needs**', include the executions of any dissidents or*

"persons of enemy of birth" or their religions or the lack of religions? Would these people just disappear like other countries of god?

The Secretary of **Defense** shall designate not fewer than 6 **military** installations as sites,,,

*The trouble with the military building these FEMA camps is to fall on many levels of disturbing. The single most I struggle with is this land these camps are on,,, federal land and one would be under federal law. Meaning anything goes. The true power, the **BIG 3** could move undetected here and remove any one perceived as a threat like you or me. We know about Guantanamo Bay and this Christian American run torture death camp on foreign soil, but if true, why don't we know about the other six or more on American soil authorized under this Bill?*

H.R. 390
January 23, 2013

This bill looks to say much the same thing as H.R.645, but is to include new wording such as "housing for individuals and families dislocated due to an emergency,,," (manmade?). This bill uses the **Superior Body's** division of the United States and this law seems to be just to provide the money for these camps while adding more justification.

However, these camps have been built before 911 and, as I understand, started in 1999. A letter I found allegedly from the Department of the Army dated January 6, 1997, uses such words as **"Civilian Inmate Labor Program"** and **"Civilian Prison Camps"** and was sent to a United States Senator.

On March 24, 1997, a member of Congress allegedly wrote a letter entitled **"civilian inmate labor program and civilian <u>prison camps</u>"**

I also found a FEMA form called **"Labor Camp Site Inspection Form"** and the form number is OSH-000X, prepared on 05/21/2008. For our good these camps have been built all over the United States and there is one near you,,, now.

*It should be understood that I cannot verify these letters or this form or these camps, but knowing how this **paranoid** secret Christian government must work, it is plausible to me. If these camps are real, why hide them? If they're just for all our good, we should look on them with pride, but because they are hidden from sight,,, can't be good.*

Now I would just like to know what emergency is this government preparing for? Could this be why Ebola could come into America without anyone doing anything to stop it? We sent planes to pick up the Christian doctors that got sick with this deadly disease and permitted it,,, no almost welcomed it to this country with open, unprotected arms.

From the outside it looks like the **deity** of **The BIG 3** finally got what they wanted,,, Ebola!!! Was an Ebola outbreak in America to be the start of the implementation of **Martial Law and the use of the 10 Regions of the Superior Body?** For them, finally, the end of America and its freedoms that just get in the way of the **BIG 3**.

Death Trains?

It has been rumored that FEMA has ordered **train box cars and shackles with guillotines** in them. Now this is a lot to absorb,,, give me a break,,, guillotines!!! But what I can find seems to be, for the most part, the same wording from multiple sources and always with a Christian organization warning of death camps and death trains. But this government is now operating under such secrecy and the Secretary of Homeland Security has a blank check for "**other appropriate needs**" so one must keep an open mind, *as opposed to a closed religious mind.* There are stories out there about FEMA ordering 102 boxcars and shackles and a sighting on (May 6, 2011) as well as others across America, but I can find no other information.

Not surprising,,, for who among us would be looking? Will Edward Snowden's next news release be of plans to remove Americans from their homes as we did in WWII? The Nazis killed millions of people in death camps right under the noses of the neighboring people and reportedly no one knew.

Some of the Christians are afraid the trains and the death camps are for them but the law gives **"faith-based"** organizations a place within the confines of each one of these camps. Well what better way to get you in under their complete control. *So maybe the Christians are right and the death camps are for them. But I think not.*

"Capture, Initial Detention and Screening", (from an unnamed document found on the internet) would seem to be the advantage of such a train for FEMA or another branch of this government. Excerpts from this document included these references: "4-58 Movement of detainees by rail is rare" and "before boarding detainees" are quotes found with "Figure 4-6. Movement by rail".

*Parts of the only information I could find. But the government has used rail to move **persons of enemy of birth** (as well as religious) in the past in Christian America as in Christian Nazi Germany. The paranoia grows on all sides.*

As I said this information is the only bits I could find at this time and it offers us a window into what this government is thinking. **"Capture"**, who and why? **"Initial"** the beginning and **"Detention"** suggested prison! **"Screening"** for what or from what and how?

I was under the assumption that we Americans were protected from such things by the constitution but if you pay attention, that has been slipping away right before our eyes. I have not made a study of all the Executive Orders created by each president but this power to circumvent all branches of the federal government,,, can't be good.

Such self imposed power, given to one person may not be devastating with this president, but what of the next? It only takes one wacko full of self grandeur like Christian Hitler and it is all over but the ovens and smoke stacks.

*But that is not likely to happen unless Simon Bar Legree the **Deity** of **The BIG 3** gives the big nod. Or has he already and these death plants are up and running now?*

Rex 84 stands for **Readiness Exercise 1984** developed by the United States government to suspend the constitution and declare **MARTIAL LAW.** Military commanders will be installed in place of elected leaders and our state and local governments will become a thing of the past. Large numbers of American citizens that are deemed to be a **"national security threats"** will be detained. And all it will take is for the president of the United States to declare a **"State of National Emergency"**. Seems we are just one step removed from having some wacko military nut job seeking total control over every aspect of our lives, forced upon us, as our remaining freedoms are taken away. People you know will just disappear. *Now remember, it's for our own good.*

Guillotines?

It is my understanding that Dr. Guillotine created a head chopping machine to be a more humane means of dealing with all the capital punishment of the French Revolution in 1789 and much to the dismay of the English aristocracy. Reportedly France stopped using the Guillotine (publicly) in 1977.

Adolf Hitler in Nazi Germany (a good Christian) reportedly used the guillotine over 16,000 times in government ordered executions from 1933 to 1945. After Germany was divided up by the powers of that time, East Germany, under The Ministry for State Security or Stasi, used the Guillotine from 1950 until the wall came down 1989 and they were no more.

I came across a story about the United States of America buying **30,000 Guillotines** and storing them in two American states. Other stories about training men on military bases, to use these killing machines, on American citizens are out there. *True or not, I don't know, but when a government conceals its actions from its people, one must ask. And if true,,,???*

The **Georgia House of Representatives** in 1995/1996 sessions allegedly passed a law,,, **HB 1274 – Death Penalty; guillotine provisions**, "a bill to be entitled an act", "article 2 of chapter 10 of title 17", "to provide for death by guillotine".

That was something I did not hear on the national news. I wonder why nothing has been reported on this new government law. Looks to me like a **test case law** to get the public used to this newest form of government death. And yet I can find no one that is publicly talking on this point. *Maybe I need to look harder or those that spoke up were the first test case.*

It should be noted I found a brand name boldly stamped on the side of one of the imagines of the guillotine and however hard I tried I could not find anything on this manufacturer. ***Nothing!!!***

I was surprised to even find a photo of a new guillotine of any type on the Christian American controlled internet and yet it was there for all to see. Yet as a manufacturer of one of the newest state of the art guillotines, this company was not out there marketing their product.

Plastic Coffins? Disposable Coffins?

Now this is disturbing. I have found a lot of information regarding the federal government or **"FEMA ordering one billion dollars worth of disposable coffin liners"**. Some reports state it is for some type of a natural disaster, (Ebola?) but I have seen these plastic coffins set next to guillotines conveniently placed there to catch the beheaded body of its victim.

I have found lots of images of piles of these government coffins stacked 20 to 30 high covering what looks like acres of land. Piled in neat stacks next to a road, behind a fence for all to see, were piles of these new black coffins with caps each claiming to comfortably hold 3 to 4 bodies.

Some of what look to be millions of these FEMA coffins have a similar design to what I found to be **Air seal Vaults** used to cover the newly departed and prevent water from entering the coffin and aiding in the decomposition.

Regardless of its original designed purpose, the question we all seem to be wondering is, why would the government want coffin covers? Unless it is to have a dual purpose and hold the newly dead. And who are these newly dead to be?

Paranoia

Just who is more paranoid,,, we American citizens or the federal government or the **Superior Body**? I believe and I fear it is none of the above. It is the dreaded **Deity** of **The BIG 3**, Simon Bar Legree who is pulling all the strings, fearing discovery and loss of control.

H.R. 645 is but one bill that refers to the **"Establishment of National Emergency Centers"**

to be run by **FEMA**. It is claimed these centers are to help us in times of emergency such as natural disasters and a platform to ensure "**faith based organizations**" will have a safe (from the boogeyman) place to pray.

If they're built for our good (as claimed), then why are there two fences surrounding these FEMA concentration camps with a layer of barbwire facing the inside? Clearly they are to keep people in,,, not keep people out (but who?). One on the list is clearly all faith based organizations and the wire is preventing these god people from getting out. Maybe they're right to be paranoid.

*We all know Simon the Deity of the **BIG 3** uses the Christians so he would want to save the leaders of such organizations. For it is how the Deity controls the masses. So it should be clear to us all, if you are Christian you will most likely not see the government guillotine. It's the rest of us that need to worry.*

Edward Snowden did report on all the spying this government does on us Americans and it was reported by him, if I have it right, that there are massive recording systems and stations to hold every word we say on the phone and every key stroke of our keyboard and internet inquiry,,, without a court order.

The phone you use has become a record of your entire life and all this information is now in the hands of the federal government,,, but why? Is their **paranoia** so intense that they fear everyone in this country or is it about control? Or is it more likely their fear is based on the history of their actions becoming public knowledge and this is the root of their paranoia.

Is this new phone that you can't remove the battery a good thing or is it a government mandate to ensure they can turn on your phone at any time to watch or listen in on everything you say when you are not on the phone? Is this the government chip to keep track of everyone and replace the dollar?

Think, you don't get paid with a check, you do all your banking,,, online and you do much of your buying,,, online and you never see your money. You have a pile of credits and at anytime this government can just take them all away and you are on the outside looking in,,, how do you eat? Such control over people would only value someone like Simon the Deity.

It is reported that 40% of the population of this country has a smart phone (not me). Close to 50% of you have given away your rights and now are monitored,,, daily. But why? I am willing to bet most of you are good people, so why would Simon Bar Legree, the Deity of the **BIG 3,** be wanting to track good people? Paranoia, control!

The 85 richest people in the world own the same amount of wealth as 3.5 billion people. This disparity could be the big one of Simon's paranoias.

As the rich get richer and the poor get poorer at some point the poor will rise up and strike back. Is that why it is rumored that someone over the **Superior Body** ordered the ten regions to be built? Is that why FEMA has created concentration camps,,, for the educated and the poor.

I can hear Simon Bar Legree the **Deity** of **The BIG 3** telling the other 84 people, "We don't want smart people on the streets of America (Cambodia Khmer Rouge) pointing out things,,, causing dissent,,, we want uneducated people (leave no child behind) that we can control with God."

The question should be as you think about this, are you on the list for camps because you are educated or the wrong religion or have the wrong color skin or are a person of enemy of birth?

It would seem most countries have built concentration camps all over the world,,, but for whom and under whose orders? Yes we know of the old ones in countries like Germany and the ones I have covered that are in the United States but what about the old ones you did not know of like Argentina, Cambodia, Italy, Japan, Russia, Chile, Yugoslavia (now called Serbia and Montenegro), Spain, North Korea and yes,,, Canada, England, Sweden and Ireland. The scary part is this is just a small list of the ones we know of,,, not a list of the new secret government concentration death camps.

To date this year November, 2014, Oklahoma has had a record number of earthquakes causing millions of dollars in damage. Many believe this alarming number of quakes is caused by hydraulic fracturing but more believe it is how these mega corporations disposed of the unwanted unknown toxic chemicals underground in disposal wells. All so they (oil) can get as many **god/notes** as they can, leaving the trash for the rest of us to clean up,,, if we ever can.

November 16, 2014, it was reported that the government is tracking you that have smart phones via planes that are equipped with what is called a "Dirtbox". A system of five planes that will track every citizen in America,,, to find the bad ones. Then of course they discard information on you good ones so don't worry. It's just big brother.

Closing Statement

Clearly something is going on that we don't see and the American people are being protected from the truth or the truth is being protected from the American people. If one person wanted to take over the United States of America,,, the platform to dictate orders to the Goyim, slaves and underlings is well built. A generation of de-educated children are ready to orderly step into place with their chips deeply implanted, giving up total control of their lives and their freedoms. Never knowing what was given to them and never knowing what was taken away.

Global Financial Super Heating

Severe weather patterns are starting to cross the globe and we all know something is not right as the last of the glaciers melt before our eyes. The great air conditioners of the planet will soon all be gone and we will see heating of the planet on a larger than biblical scale. Regions of the world will see mass migrations of people fleeing starvation, desperately trying to save themselves and their children. Killing of all people that worship the wrong religion, the wrong god, will be a daily event, hunted down and murdered with such joy from all sides,,, as they are now.

Some that know better than I believe that we are but one step away from total financial chaos in the world. It is because we put our faith in the almighty **god/notes** that cover the planet like a death shroud. If you put your trust and faith in these slips of ground up trees, you will have a lot of company for much of the world has done just that.

When the **god/notes** are found out to have no value, air travel with be a thing found only in our memories,,, stories told by the old ones to help pass the daytime while we hide from the suns heat on this ever heating planet. The full effects of Global Shading will be crossing the planet in a short amount of time as governments try to put back the pollution from the big planes high in the sky,,, now gone with your dollar's value.

Global Financial Super Heating

The ones responsible for this catastrophic disaster are closer than you may think. For they are all around us going about their lives as though things will go on like this forever. It is in their silence that the string master, Simon Bar Legree the **Deity** of the **Big 3**, the true power, lives and as we all say nothing he and his henchmen grow stronger and stronger, every day becoming more powerful.

Knowledge is a powerful thing if you are smart enough to use it. But what can one person do? The following is a list of recommendations that may help take some power from the rich.

1. Stop giving power, (money) to these super rich corporations. Examples: do you need to buy a cup of coffee from one super rich company? Can you live without a phone sold by a super rich company, which tracks your every move for the government? Do you have to eat fast food giving dollars to another super power or can you get up earlier and eat at home or a local restaurant and keep the money in the local economy?

2. If you make $1,000.00 per week don't spend $1,200.00 per week. Once you have your spending under control invest in tangibles like gold or silver, hedging your bets on the crash of the **god/notes**. This is going to happen as it has in the past,,, it's just paper.

3. Education is a powerful tool and with exposing these criminals guilty of sex abuse of a child and genocide will help push them and their ignorance back into their **priest holes** where they belong,,, hiding and a part of the dark past. They have a death grip on the world and we, the ignorant, give them power over us,,, and they take it gladly.

4. One religious terrorist organization has slowly moved into federal and state government as well as local governments and if no one will stand up to defend this once free land, shortly the clocks will be turning back to the dark ages. We have the power to destroy by exposing these giants of evil with their own weapons of self destructions,,, **dishonesty, felony, and embarrassment**.

5. Clearly these governments and religions are merely tools of some master plan, coming from and through the **Superior Body.** But is there time to expose it and do something about it? I fear anyone that tries, will face the same fate as Julian Assange and Edward Snowden and of course John F. Kennedy.

The end of 2014

Reportedly, the news accounts I can find, within the past 10 years of record keeping, 9 of those 10 years, we on the planet have seen new records met and passed. 2014 was the hottest year since record keeping going back to the 1880s.

At the same time the world's ocean temperatures are also passing previous highs as everything gets hotter and hotter.

There are more jets flying people all over the globe and polluting the upper atmosphere this year of 2014 and that action should have helped drive the temperature down,,, not up as I understand **Global Shading**. This temperature rise tells me it would have been a much hotter year, if those jets for the rich would not have been up there.

Think of it this way, take a glass of water filled with ice and put it out in the sun on a hot summer day. As the ice melts the water remains cool until most of the ice slowly melts in the sun. Then when it is all gone the water gets very hot. We all need those glaciers. We all need those rain forests. And when I say we all,,, I mean every living thing.

Global Financial Super Heating is one **god/note** crash away - like the reported 50% drop in value of the Russian dollar this year (2014) may be the start.

Simon Bar Legree

UNDER ONE GOD

William J. Ryan copyright © 2013 #027

The God/Note....

The True God Almighty!

Mafia Family Structure

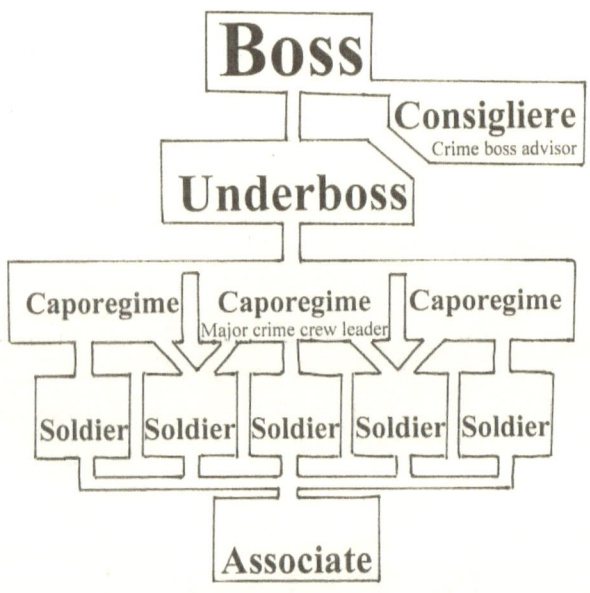

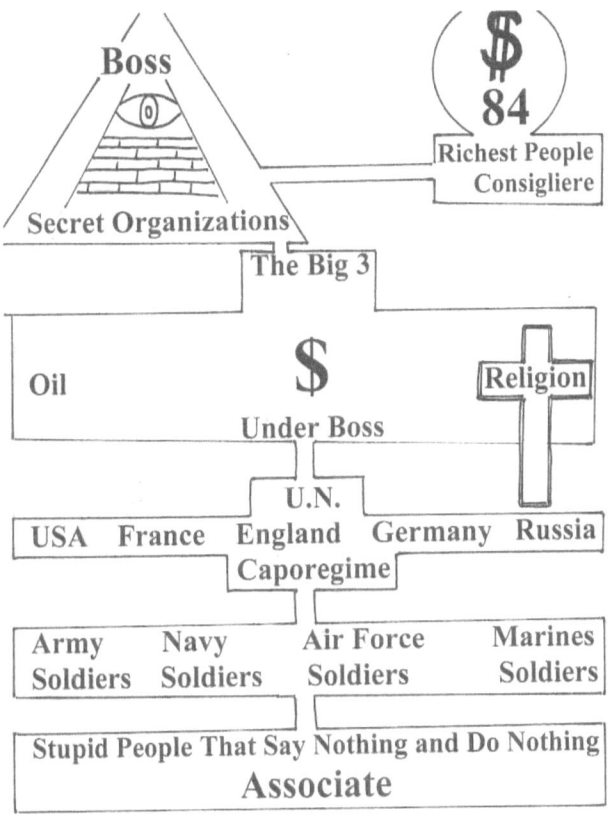

Example of how Mafia Family Structure could apply to world governing powers and their turf wars using all people (religious) to make money.

Global Financial Super Heating

William J. Ryan
Post Office Box 666
Dade City, FL. 33526

December 31, 2014

To whom may be concerned,

This is an open letter to the reader. I wish to make it clear that if it should be reported that I took my own life in some type of suicide I wish to make the following statement.

I in no way committed suicide and my death is a murder to silence my dissenting voice and to stop me from openly speaking of subjects that these people prefer not be spoken of. They have done their best to stay in the back rooms out of the limelight pulling all the strings, committing genocide for one god or another, love of money and power over all people.

If my body is found hanging from a tree in my back yard with 27 bullet holes in my back and the government declared my death to be the strangest case of suicide they have ever seen, just know it is a lie.

Sincerely,

William J. Ryan

WANTED

Simon Bar Legree

Wanted for genocide, war crimes, murder, drug dealing and protecting pedophiles

Global Financial Super Heating

Dictionary
Terms and their hidden meanings

Al Qaeda: a terrorist organization like Christianity

American interests: a term given by the spin master to provide misinformation regarding large corporate financial investments, profits and/or gains, all guarded by young American blood.

Amnesty: 1) an act of desperation (by those in power), 2) to circumvent certain laws and render them invalid as needed to protect the powerful.

Anarchy: a result when laws are not enforced

Autodidacticism: autodidactism, autodidact, 1) self-directed learning, 2) self-education

Bad Ink: news reports of a negative nature.

Balance War: 1) a means to ensure the longevity of war to enhance profits, 2) opposite of quick and decisive.

Bankruptcy: a maneuver endorsed by the federal government, to gain profit for attorneys and other members of the legal justice system by using others financial misfortune. *Other countries use accountants to handle this,,, go figure.*

Bankster: 1) unprosecuted person within the banking industry that commits fraud or other criminal acts associated with lending, the mortgage trade, illegal commerce, stock exchanges, etc. 2) above the law, 3) protected by Christians.

Blue Gold: drinking water

Global Financial Super Heating

Bribe: political campaign contribution.

Change: a form of currency that gives the illusion of value

Chaos: ever eroding pillar government sits upon to avoid the outcome of the future and what it helped to make.

Christian: 1) a religion stolen from the Jews whereby they worship a bastard Jew executed criminal man   2) a religion that protects pedophiles at the highest level, the pope   3) a terrorist organization that permits killing across the globe

Citizen Terrorist: people that openly complain while working in the death camps.

CONOP 8888: reportedly, an elaborate plan created by the U.S. Strategic Command (Pentagon) to counter an attack by an apocalypse zombie (the walking dead) outbreak.

D.D.D.: Drug Dealing Doctors.

D.O.O.M.: Devaluing Of Our Money

Dark money: a term given to **god/notes** that are untraceable and used to buy influence and power over other people in power.

Department of Disinformation: an elusive branch of the federal and state governments used to create and disseminate false statements and misleading information to the public.

Election Process: in America there is only one party (the rich) divided into two parts, Republican Democrat

Global Financial Super Heating

Freedom Fighters: a term given to U.S. armed forces to justify invading other countries for their land, water or wealth.

God/note: 1) an illusion of safety 2) trick by those in power to give legitimacy 3) phony, fake, counterfeit, false, fraud, hoax, sham, etc.

Gods of Prey: imaginary deities created by those wanting a free ride in life, taking advantage of the weak and frightened. Afraid to live, afraid to die.

GOTT MITUNS: German for 'God is with us' found on WWII belt buckles.

Goyim: 1) all people that are not Jewish 2) cattle 3) of no value 4) put on earth to serve the chosen ones

Greener Lands: places filled with low intelligence people that the **BIG 3** and take advantage of.

Inflation: a mythical explanation for the de-valuation of any paper currency resulting in higher prices and decreases in purchasing power

Insurance Fraud: happens when you buy insurance and the carrier refuses to pay a claim.

Jew: a religion where only their people will go to heaven and the rest of us are Goyim not permitted in their land

Mirror: 1) a place for the vane to relish themselves, 2) the worst invention man ever made

Moral Compass: 1) an ethical conscience that politicians do not possess, but pretend to. 2) a thing lacking in all religions

N.A.T.O.: Nations Access To Oil

Nicotine: 1) an addictive drug purchased freely without a prescription 2) and additive drug added to cigarettes to make them more addictive and profitable to the drug dealers, cigarettes manufacturers, 3) a narcotic like cocaine sold freely by Christian law makers and with their blessing

Occupiers: 1) freedom fighters, 2) armies of domestic and foreign corporate criminals who take over and rule our country via the government, 3) Christians

One Party: in Christian America the election system is but one party of the rich divided in to two parts, the Republicans and the Democrats.

P.B. People: a natural occurrence in all species of life found primarily within ants called Poliergus Breviceps. Slave masters.

P.O.P.E.: Protector Of Pedophiles Everywhere

Persons of enemy of birth: paranoid reaction to war permitting war crimes by a government against its own people.

Planned Obsolescence: a global business model that follows the premise of, "let's make all the cash we can now and let someone else pay to clean up the mess.

Plastic People: people of the plastic age of pollution, poisoning, and other destruction of the planet – modern man.

Poli-Christian: 1) an elected official that pretends to be a Christian for the purpose of getting elected and then violates their Christian values 2) the anti-Christ 3) type A personality of destruction.

Political system in America: a single governing body of the rich divided into two parts, Republican and Democrat

Politician: 1) guardian of major corporations, 2) person willing to do anything for paper money

Religion and Ethics: a newsweekly program on PBS that is allegedly an oxymoron.

Scrupulosity: 1) a psychological disorder 2) a madness that takes over the mind 3) an infectious mental delusion 4) mass hypnoses

Selection Process: term describing the election process when large corporations buy (with campaign contributions) both sides of a ballot (all candidates)

Separation of church and state: 1) the First Amendment to the constitution of the United States, 2) antiquated term used by Thomas Jefferson and atheists, 3) fallacy, 4) false premise and unforeseeable law, per the Christians.

Shark Market: 1) a place where you take your hard earned money, give it to strangers and they make fees off of you when that need cash 2) those who don't make money, but take money.

Simon Bar Legree: 1) a fictitious character made up by the writer of this book, 2) reprehensive, or representative of a real person unseen by the masses, 3) the darkest level of power any living human can obtain, 4) satan that has tricked religious people to kill so he can control them.

Global Financial Super Heating

Social Security Administration: the office that oversees the federal government's Ponzi scheme.

Speaking in tongues: 1) the art of speaking to God, 2) language of idiots, 3) created to fool the masses and take their money

Spin: lies created to mislead and deceive the public.

String Master: 1) title given to unseen corporate leaders (aka, puppeteers) who controls elected employees, 2) mafia, a thing per the FBI that does not exist

Subsidies: welfare for the rich.

Superior Body: 1) a governing organization that Christian America must report to, 2) a corrupt group of world leaders bought by the top 85 people in the world, 3) the United Nations or UN

Super Hyper-Devaluation: 1) a thing that happens to all paper money or god/notes, 2) often called high inflation however there is no such thing as inflation, 3) end result of a poorly run country usually for god 4) a people or race stripped clean by the **BIG 3** that know what they are doing.

White Gold: china from China

Global Financial Super Heating

I am always surprised by the gullibility of people of god that will follow anyone and justify their actions of murder, rape, enslavement and stealing, in God's name. But they should know how they look to someone on the outside looking in. To the best of my knowledge, all religions do this but I have singled out one that has taken over this country.

God or Satan

by W. J. Ryan

A god made everything in six days and came to earth and made man in his image, only he forgot woman and apparently after building everything ran out of magic dust so without anesthesia, this god, ripped a rib out of Adam's chest and tossed it in the dirt, where the first man now bleeding profusely in agonizing pain, saw a women grow before him as he must have been passing out from the pain. This unmarried couple propagated and covered the earth with bastard children,
God or Satan?

A man comes through a window at night and rapes a virgin called Mary, gets her pregnant on the first try and becomes a dead beat dad never helping raise the bastard child,
God or Satan?

The bastard child of this rapist god, allegedly could turn good drinking water into intoxicating alcohol called wine,

God or Satan?

The bastard child, without a father's guidance gets into trouble, breaking the Jewish law of the land and his crime carries a capital death sentence and he is executed as a criminal next to a thief,

God or Satan?

Per the teachings of the rapist godfather, it's ok to own slaves,,, as long as you do not covet your neighbors' slaves,

God or Satan?

Hundreds of thousands of women entering this cult and dedicating their lives to one of these almighty beings, must marry this dead Jew bastard executed criminal, committing a sin under their rapist god called bigamy,

God or Satan?

Once a year, to stay in good standings each members of this satanic cult must eat the flesh of their executed dead bastard criminal Jew man and drink his blood,

God or Satan?

Women rank at the same level as sinful homosexuals and when Pope **Joan** had her abstinence baby in the street, in or about 1335, her death was soon to follow from the hands of an angry mob of members of the cult. To this day members of this cult avoids the spot of her murder and the Christian abortion committed that day and the parade takes a back street,

God or Satan?

Murdering crusades in their leaders' names, reaped ill-gained riches and to this day gold stained with the blood of its true owners,,, adorns their highest temples ceilings,

God or Satan?

Following the teachings of this executed criminal Jew man-god, in the 1400s, a government created the first international drug cartel, spreading its devastating deadly addiction to China for worldly wealth,,, white gold,

God or Satan?

In the 1500s a different government controlling its people under this criminal Jew man-god, invaded the new land (South America) enslaving its people, seizing its wealth and chopping off the arms of thousands of those who would not pray to this earthly criminal,

God or Satan?

Adolf Hitler, a follower of the teachings of this criminal Jew man-god, believed he had the God given right to kill all Jews because they killed this new Jew man-god and from the words of three small kids from South America one of their saints said to them *"invade Russia and God will be on your side."* And he did,,, killing millions,

God or Satan?

Thousands of years have gone by and the followers of an executed criminal Jew man from the dark ages, are still waging wars, killing all who would stand up against their supreme earthly leader, one of several,

God or Satan?

November 22, 1963 president John F. Kennedy was murdered and some people believe it was the war mongers because he was ending the Vietnam War. Others believe it was the Christians' leaders that ordered his death because he was stopping this Christian crusade in that country,

God or Satan?

September 11, 2001 around 8:50am that the first airplane was driven into the first tower in New York and about 9:05am the second plane followed driven by people of a different god and president George W. Bush does not act surprised by the first attack or the second attack on the WTC. Some think this was part of a 911Christian plot,

God or Satan?

Since the end of WWII the Christians have been moving all the Jews to the promised land, stealing this land from the Palestinian people and thereby putting them all (the Jews) in one place on earth surrounded by their enemies and this American Christian led government sells 600 billion dollars worth of lethal arms to their hated enemies that have vowed to kill all the Jews,,, the Muslims,

God or Satan?

The highest ranking human religious leader (standing next to their gods) of this cult, stands before his people as their leader to guide them to the promised land and the next life,,, **protects pedophiles,,,** child rapists found within their highest order of teaching,

God or Satan?

It has been alleged by some of the faithful of this cult, that the images of the victim of Gods rape,,, Mary,,, has been seen to cry tears of blood.

Is there any question why?

I am reminded of the words of one very good and brutal Christian that did his best to spread the lunacies of God.

"make the lie BIG, make it simple, keep saying it, and eventually they will believe it."

Adolf Hitler

What Would They Say?

By William J. Ryan

May 27, 2014
Memorial Day

As a relatively poor kid growing up in the midwest of the United States I lived an idyllic Mayberry life and did not know it. The air was clean and safe to breath, the sky was blue and you could eat the food and drink the water. There were no drugs, no gangs, no race riots and there were half as many people and they were friendlier. I was the third and unwanted child of two distance parents that should never have had children and they hated each other. So understandably I was drawn to older people looking up to them for some kind of guidance. I did not know how good that pool of people was.

My earliest pleasant memories are of playing on the front porch by myself and saying hi to the people walking by and some were singing or the lost art of whistling. Think hard now, when is the last time you heard someone whistling? They, for the most part, were friendly to this dirty faced, unloved, little boy looking up to them. I was certain something was wrong with me for my parents rejected me as well as others,,, all but the veterans from WWII. My guess is they had seen lots of dirty faced little kids on the streets of Europe, so it did not bother them and they could look past dirt and see the smile.

Our butcher was a big friendly man just down the street and I remember looking up to him in his old unpainted store with bare wooden floors and the smell of blood filled the air. One day I asked him about the tattoo on his arm and he showed it to me and told me he was a survivor of the concentration camps. I was too small to remember all the stories he told me but I was drawn to this person from another country and the war he lived through and the people that helped him. He loved this country and all Americans.

I remember asking adults if they were in that war and if they had time they would tell me their stories. I was drawn to these people even more. I recall it hitting closer to home when I asked about the stars in the windows of some of the homes near us and I was told, those families lost a son in the war. One gold star for each child lost. A shroud of death seemed to cover their house as I would seldom see those people living within.

A few blocks away from our house was the local school and I would walk the same street each day to go to school. One day I noticed one of the unmaintained homes that I passed every day. The house was dirty the lawn uncut and the bushes over grown blocking the sidewalk. I remember wanting to yell at someone in the house to cut their bushes that were blocking my way, but never saw anyone. Then I knew why their yard was unkempt,,, there were four gold stars stitched to a faded blue cloth hanging in the window facing the street. I stood there for some time thinking how each gold star was a son that had given his life so all of us could be free. The ones left in this house had given all they could give and did not care what things looked like, for they were drained. For me intense sadness draped this house that had stopped in time.

I collected as many stories as I could from these men and women and loved to watch the old black and white war movies from that time. One news reel recounted how a news crew, that came in after D day, the Normandy Day Invasion. The officer in charge emotionally told how a female reporter, that had pointed to the red sand beach and said something like, "oh they have the same red beaches we have back home." And the officer turned quickly to her and snapped back, "that is not red sand,,, that's American blood!" and it was there before them for miles.

My respect and thirst for understanding the Greatest Generation continues to this day. Whenever I would meet one of these vets, I would get them to tell me stories until they had to go or could talk no more. The last WWII vet I spoke to fought with

Audie Murphy (the most decorated soldier of WWII) and since our meeting he has passed on. (I shook the hand that shook the hand of Audie Murphy) I am the lucky one for I got to shake his hand and thank this man for my freedom. As an adult I did sincerely thank every one of these vets I spoke to.

It's only now that I, as an old man, think I may know what made all those great and brave people the Greatest Generation. The war effort to win this war was instilled in every person and ran all the way to the top.

Adolf Hitler, a good Christian was sure he had God on his side and wanted revenge on the Jews that had killed his God. (Jewish Deicide) He wanted only good Christians in his ranks as he (Like George) invaded countries that had done nothing to him. I can't imagine what it would have been like to march innocent men, women and children off to their deaths because God tells me it is right. Most said, *"I was just under orders."* The rest of their lives they had to live with what they did,,, all for God's sakes.

After WWII the war mongers liked all the money they had made and wanted to keep it going so they invented new weapons and found new enemies to fight. The REDs were a hot button for years mostly because they were a godless people that felt government should take care of everyone equally without God,,, so let's go kill them.

France wanted their colonies (Vietnam) back. After the Japanese returned home France stepped back in and got covert help from the American government saving Christians. Soon the war machine was back in business and then came Korea. Neither country had done anything to us, and yet we invaded, killed and left our blood on their soul.

Then came the cold war and prayer in school and anti-abortionists and God was everywhere and appeared on our money. For me this god thing ended when I was watching an old black and white movie about how the devil and its followers had to "drink the blood and eat the flesh of Satan" and that ended God for me for these two were the same. I will not and have not ever drunk any blood or ate any flesh from either side nor will I.

At this same time we helped move all the Jews into one place and set them down next to their enemies that to this day surround them on all sides. Only American dollars protect these holy people as they wage war on their new neighbors, stealing their land. This new Jewish state takes whatever it wants and kills anyone that gets in its way as Christian Americans stand behind them. Seems they have God on their side (gott mit uns) and can do whatever they want to the non Jews or Goyim, firing up all the surrounding enemies.

We seem to have our nose and hands in every ones business and there is no end to the involvement of the policemen of the world,,, America,,, spreading their good Christian values. And once more it crosses the globe like a plague complete with torture and silent killing machines that strike down innocent people from the sky. In this country we now have secret courts and secret prisons and to this day (in America) allegedly incarcerate people without trials.

George W. Bush, a proclaimed born again Christian, then invades a country that did nothing to us. Our American soldiers are called on to fight and kill people in a country that committed no crime against us. Seems they just had oil or we had to use up all those bombs or allegedly Bush had plans to invade Iraq because,,, per George "he tried to kill my daddy."

Now we know what happened to the Greatest Generation, they were replaced with the Christians. John F. Kennedy was the first Catholic president and now you can't get into office unless you cow down to this the king of evil, controlling us all.

The men that led us into the battle of WWII had total commitment to end the brutality of war quickly by throwing everything at the war we had. But we did not do that in the Korean war, we did not do that in the Vietnam War and we are not doing that now. We are doing what I call a **Balanced War**. This will ensure the perpetuation of one or several wars across the globe to ensure the consumption of our war production.

Adolf Hitler invaded countries that had done nothing to him just as America has done the same thing. George and Adolf have that and Christianity in common. Our freedom fighters, those young brave men and women are asked to serve repeatedly in these modern day Christian crusades. We take the spoils of war,,, OIL,,, and spread the word of this Christian God,,, the true goal.

Only these Americans are not welcomed with open arms by the inhabitants of these countries. Instead they are viewed like Hitler's men must have been greeted, with hatred, disdain and viewed as heretic invaders and occupiers, forcing their god on them. And now these, our boys, must return home carrying the images of war and something much worse, the images of an occupier just like the German solders did at the end of their reign.

Is there any wonder why so many American soldiers have taken their own lives once they return home? You can call them whatever you want, freedom fighters, is not how the indigenous people of those countries look at or call these invaders and occupiers. Is there any question as to why they hate us so much and strike out at us from every point they can across the globe?

I lay this at the feet of all Christians that look the other way and accept that this is God's will. Separation of church and state in the beginnings of the United States was understood and pushed hard by Thomas Jefferson and others with a full and personal understanding of the value of a *"wall of separation between church and state."* The Supreme Court has thrown out the first amendment to the constitution of the United States. It is no more and I wonder, **what would they say?**

As I look back on my life I know now I was very lucky to have known these people from the Greatest Generation. Their stories come racing back into my mind as I think of each one I knew. Everyone is now dead and gone and I can't help but wonder, **what would they say?**

It was reported that this Christian led government made 50 strikes to kill Saddam Hussein and missed 50 times. But they killed innocent men, women and children trying. The one that keeps coming back into my mind is the 50th try and how a house was pointed out by an informant as the house that held Saddam and without checking,,, those good Christians destroyed it with a bomb from the air.

Picking through the rubble of this, that once was a home, they found a dead woman and her two dead little girls. The husband was at work. Could they not have found another way? Would those men from the Greatest Generation have done the same thing? Could they not have just knocked on the door and asked? Would those from the Greatest Generation carry out that order to bomb another home killing more innocent people? **What would they say?**

This Christian government crosses the globe picking up people and kidnapping them and taking them to other countries to be tortured. How is this right? Apparently it can only be right if you are Christian. How does God empower you with that right? Seems this god will forgive you if you do something wrong and you ask for forgiveness. Just ask and you can do anything you want to anyone you want. No earthly retribution. And we see this in all aspects of this Christian led government. No war profiteers go to jail, no bankers go to jail, no poli-Christian go to jail, and this criminal led religion covers up the crimes of pedophiles found within their ranks and no one is prosecuted. **What would they say?**

Barack Obama, another good Christian, has authorized the sale of 600 billion dollars (if I have the number right) worth of fighter jets and other war machine to be sold to the arch enemies of the Jews.

Why would they do such a thing other than to enrich the war mongers and aid in the perpetuation of war? I can only think of one, the Christians have armed the enemies of their enemies so they can kill each other as they are in Syria. The Jews killed the Christian god and are now poised to see their enemies coming at them with all manner of warring power,,, brought to you by Christian America. Christians have armed both sides of their enemies. **What would they say?**

U. S. dollars are given to Pakistan because that is how we make friends,,, we buy them. It worked well as a child so it should work well as a grown up,,, right. The Pakistani government does not like Christian Americans but likes their money so they take it and give much to Al Qaeda to buy war machinery from the war profiteers that cross the globe freely. Americans are funding both sides of this religious war, and no one goes to jail.

What would they say?

Ren-di-tion: /ren'diSHen 1.) performance of a piece of music or dramatic role 2.) sending foreign terrorist to a country for torture.

Planting Flowers
By
William J. Ryan

I looked up a word today
One I think has gone astray

A word that once held such beauty
Now is used for patriot duty

We all do stand in perfect rows
Silent voices all in neat knows

Rendition once held reproduction of splendor
Now it holds visions of crushing dissenters

The religious rejoice with such glee
Their towers of God rise up for all to see

Rape torched killing all the same
As we permit the arranging of our brains

Looking past the people that once were here
We all that think, look forward with much fear

333

Global Financial Super Heating

Trying his best and defending his land
The life force energy once a man

Now lies silent for stepping out of line
His words, deeds and actions now part of the brine

Plants struggle through the warm earth
Bringing us all joy as they burst

Dead dissenters terrorist them all
Now feeding the flowers to help them grow tall

I can't begin to explain where this came from. I was watching the evening news when the first line came into my head. I hit the mute button and two minutes later it was done. The mind is a wondrous thing. I constantly explore diligently, trying to keep all doors open to all thinking,,,come what may.

W.G.R.

Books by William J Ryan

The Extermination of Kings, Part I

Journey to the Bay of Bengal

Two Tibetan monks witness the butchering and murder by the Chinese of all the inhabitants of a monastery in the Himalayas. As the only survivors and eyewitnesses, they face starvation as they are being hunted. They head south looking for sanctuary and are struck by the countless inhumanities they see and acts of destruction to the earth they love. *Available now*

The Extermination of Kings, Part II

The Dark Continent

Word spreads of the only survivors and the monks receive help. Captain Jack, a big Irish seaman, gets them across the Indian Ocean and Ocyrus guides them across Africa through the perils they face there - man's inhumanity to man, foreign countries' trash and the consumption of all living things in order to survive. *Available SOON*

The Extermination of Kings, Part III

America

They are befriended by a billionaire that gets them to the land of the free but manipulates events for his own agenda. This is the last of the trilogy of easy to read fast-moving stories, with an outcome that helps the Tibetan's gain power. *Available SOON*

Sheriff Jessy of Boonies, Kentucky 2007 Part I

An amusing and nostalgic look at an idyllic community and what happens when it is invaded by corrupt politicians. Sheriff Jessy tries to hold the community together in spite of black money and wins in the end. *Available now*

Sheriff Jessy of Boonies, Kentucky 2009 Part II

Revenge of Dick and George, two boys from Texas

Politicians being what they are, bring an endless barrage of destruction to the community, with the goal of turning it into Lead Ville, USA. In their effort to destroy the community they expose Jessy and his dark secrets, with a tragic outcome. *Available soon*

Levi's Reverse Wave Absorption

Global Financial Super Heating

This is a riveting science fiction story about an Amish college student who invents a way to prevent earthquakes and pays for it with his life. As an FBI sting goes bad, corrupt Federal agents are exposed, taking you all the way to the top of the Government. *Available now*

First Defense

Illegal drug trafficking across civilian lands, forces a community to defend themselves as the Federal Government looks the other way. *Warning: contains shocking solutions to real problems*, like Amy and her drill. *Available now*

The Good News Show

A scintillating account, scene by scene, of the news media, the control over the airwaves of American radio and television. With the unraveling of this empire comes a hard look at the future of our planet and the destruction that is coming. *Available now*

Just Deserves

An in-depth look into life after death and the worlds beyond, from the vantage point of one who has just passed. Strange encounters and friendships develop as the earth reaches its end of domination over man. *Available now*

The Copper Pit

A dramatic tale with an unlikely result of the President's and Congress's decision to banish outlawed street gangs to an abandoned copper mine in the middle of America's desert. *Available now*

Seeds of Change

The story of a big city attorney who is forced by life events to move to a rural community which has been devastated by the Federal Government's programs like giving tax breaks to corporations that send American jobs overseas. A powerful political machine develops that changes the nation. *Available soon*

Letters to President Obama, 52 weeks 52 letters

Here is actual White House correspondence (with responses) and commentaries written by a common small-town businessman struggling in the 2010 depression. It reveals the author's transformation from a confused and frustrated citizen, to an awakened and empowered one. *Available now*

Global Financial Super Heating

Car Slugs

A disturbing look into the retail car sales industry through the eyes of one mentally over stimulated salesman. The story is set in the heyday of the 1990's, before the destruction of our country by the banking industry. *Available SOON*

Lords

The re-incarnated Incan god king, Pachacuti, attempts to educate his people in order to reverse the brain-washing that began by the Spanish in the 14th century and to retrieve what was stolen from them. Additionally, to abolish the strangle-hold of their religion, his efforts are ended as a man-made plague crosses the globe and only the rarest of human beings survive to repopulate. *Available SOON*

The 3 Ks

A murder mystery revealing how the police and prosecutors of our justice system work as they *build a case* and *make the facts fit* one particular man. *Available Soon*

Available now through Amazon.com and other fine retail book stores

www.ingramcontent.com/pod-product-compliance
Lightning Source LLC
Chambersburg PA
CBHW030418290526
45786CB00001B/39